Google

Google

Virginia Scott

Corporations That Changed the World

GREENWOOD PRESS
Westport, Connecticut • London

Library of Congress Cataloging-in-Publication Data

Scott, Virginia A.
Google / Virginia Scott.
  p. cm. — (Corporations that changed the world, 1939–2486)
  Includes bibliographical references and index.
  ISBN 978–0–313–35127–3 (alk. paper)
  1. Google (Firm)—History.   2. Internet industry—United States—
History.   I. Title.
  HD9696.8.U64G6665   2008
  338.7'6102504—dc22   2008030541

British Library Cataloguing in Publication Data is available.

Library of Congress Catalog Card Number: 2008030541
ISBN: 978–0–313–35127–3
ISSN: 1939–2486

First published in 2008

Greenwood Press, 88 Post Road West, Westport, CT 06881
An imprint of Greenwood Publishing Group, Inc.
www.greenwood.com

Printed in the United States of America

Contents

Acknowledgments

I am grateful to Jeff Olson, Senior Acquisitions Editor, Business/Management/Economics of Praeger Publishers for giving me the opportunity to write this book and for his expertise and kindness. I would also like to thank the kind, talented, and meticulous editors at Apex CoVantage. Special thanks to my sister, Missy Scott, a true inspiration, who not only helped with the book, but with all of life's challenges.

I would also like to thank the following people for their expertise and help:

Tim Cannon
Carole Leita
Sally Floyd
Tim Lederman
Chris O'Neal

And, many thanks to Google for being there as a way to search for everything under the sun.

Introduction

Google founders Larry Page and Sergey Brin struck gold with their search engine. That vein of gold just gets richer and richer.

Larry and Sergey started Google in 1999 while they were still graduate students at Stanford University. They were billionaires by 2004—at the age of 31. Google's market capitalization at the end of the first quarter of 2008 was $184 billion. Its stock, which initially sold for $85 a share, has climbed as high as over $700 in its short life. Despite market analysts' concerns that Google, like most U.S. companies, would feel the effects of the weakening U.S. economy in 2008, it showed a 30% profit in the first quarter.[1]

In the spring of 2008, Google replaced Yahoo! as the most popular Web site in the United States. What's more, Google has been named the number one company to work for by *Forbes* for two years running. This helps the company to attract the brightest young minds—called "Googlers"—which together comprise one of the best technology think tanks in the world. Larry and Sergey openly admit that the Googlers are the company's most important asset, and they nurture them in one of the most talked-about corporate cultures in the business world.

As Sergey explained in a 1999 *Washington Post* interview, the name Google was a derivative of *googol,* a mathematical term for an enormous number—1 followed by 100 zeroes. Sergey commented that he and Larry felt like it was an appropriate name because they were working with the World Wide Web, and it was enormous. Could he have known then just how enormously powerful his company would become?[2]

In a few short years, Google became a household world around the world as it became the number one destination for people searching for information on the Web. Merriam Webster added it to its dictionary in 2001, and the Oxford English Dictionary included it as a verb in 2006. One hears it used in statements such as: "I need to google that and get more background." Or "I googled him and found out that…"

How did Google become so well-known and so popular—especially considering it has never advertised? (How ironic, because it generates most of its revenue from advertising for other companies!) The answer is that it never needed to advertise. From the beginning, its users spread the word about its fast and efficient search service. Plus, many of its services are offered to users for free, which attracts users by the millions. And because Larry and Sergey remain committed to end users, the company courts them constantly in the hope they'll provide feedback and new ideas. And they do.

How did these young men and their company become so successful so quickly? How did they influence the world to such a degree that the name of their company and the act of using their search engine become a household word? How did they gain the attention of over half of the people in the world searching for information, leaving their competitors in the dust? These are some of the questions this book answers.

What started as a graduate school project with the goal of perfecting how people search for information on the World Wide Web grew into a company that shook not only the world of search but dramatically changed the worlds of advertising and communication. It changed the lives of those who use Google and who depend on it for research, news, quick answers, shopping, communication, and collaboration. It has even changed how we are able view and explore our entire planet as we marvel at and take advantage of the satellite images provided by Google Earth.

Behind Google's mission "to organize the world's information and make it universally accessible and useful" is Larry and Sergey's belief that completing or moving toward completion of this mission will make the world a better place.[3] Behind the company's motto of "Don't be evil" is the belief that one must do good in the world.[4] This belief has prompted Google in the past few years to launch an ambitious philanthropic organization that is likely to create a new standard for corporate social responsibility. Google's commitment to the "Don't be evil" motto has been questioned in relation to controversies that we'll consider. And some people fear the sheer size and power of the company and how the information it has gathered about us as we use Google might be used. Most of us, however, would be lost without Google, making it a great force for constructive progress. No one can deny: Google has changed the world.

NOTES

1. "Google Announces First Quarter 2008 Results," Investor Relations Financial Release, http://investor.google.com/releases/2008Q1.html (accessed June 22, 2008).

2. Leslie Walker, *Washington Post*.com-LIVE, November 4, 1999, http://www.washingtonpost.com/wp-srv/liveonline/business/walker/walker110499.htm (accessed March 10, 2008).

3. "Company Overview," Google Corporate Information, http://www.google.com/corporate (accessed March 12, 2008).

4. http://investor.google.com/conduct.html (accessed June 23, 2008).

Chapter One

Meet Google's Founders

How does a profitable company with a huge impact on society, like Google, come into being? There are many ingredients, but you can usually follow the roots of a company's culture and ultimate impact back to one thing: the personality and interests of the founders.

Google founders Larry Page and Sergey Brin each brought distinctive childhood experiences, educational backgrounds, social consciousness, and personality to bear on the formation of their company. At the same time, there are fascinating similarities in their backgrounds that contributed to their strong friendship and shared vision for their company when it came into being.

Both, for example, shared some experiences in their somewhat unusual childhoods. They both grew up with access to computers when computers in the home were rare. They both attended Montessori schools in their early years—an experience that would later inspire them to require their engineers to spend 20% of their work week on projects that captured their imaginations. They both were curious, smart youngsters. Both had well-educated parents whose work revolved around computing and science. Both sets of parents nurtured their sons' curiosity and encouraged them to explore and try all kinds of new things. They both ended up at Stanford—where they met—for graduate work. Now isn't that a happy coincidence? One thing led to another, and before long Google was born.

Let's take a look at the backgrounds of these remarkable partners up to the time their paths crossed.

LARRY PAGE

Lawrence Edward Page was born March 26, 1973, in Lansing, Michigan. His mother, Gloria, taught computer programming at Michigan State University. His father, Carl, was a professor of computer science and artificial intelligence at Michigan State and spent every extra penny on computers. In an October 28, 2000, interview, Larry says their house was usually a mess, with computers and *Popular Science* magazines all over the place. His love affair with computers started when he was six years old. "I just enjoyed using the stuff. It was sort of lying around, and I got to play with it." Not many people had computers just lying around the house in 1978. He was the first kid in his elementary school to turn in an assignment that was a word-processed document. Then his older brother taught him to take things apart, and it wasn't long before he was taking apart everything in the house to see how it worked. Larry admits his early access to computers and his unique childhood shaped his interests in invention, technology, and business. Early on, he also realized that he wanted to change the world.

> From a very early age, I also realized I wanted to invent things. So I became really interested in technology and also then, soon after, in business, because I figured that inventing things wasn't any good; you really had to get them out into the world and have people use them to have any effect. So probably from when I was 12, I knew I was going to start a company eventually.[1]

Larry's primary school education was at a Montessori school. He received his high school diploma from East Lansing High School in Michigan and a B.S. with honors in engineering with a concentration on computer engineering from the University of Michigan. On the university's solar car team, he continues to be committed to sustainable transportation technology. As we'll see, RechargeIT, part of Google's philanthropic effort, promotes the adoption of plug-in hybrid electric vehicles and funds related research.

When Larry traveled to California to visit Stanford University to "try it on for size," the guide for his group tour was a second-year student named Sergey Brin. Rumor has it that initially they bantered back and forth and squabbled about a wide range of subjects. But later they became friends and research colleagues at Stanford, collaborators and covisionaries who created a company that would change the world.

Larry received a master's degree in computer science from Stanford before leaving to give his full attention to Google, where he is currently president for products. In December 2007, he married Lucy Southworth, a doctoral student at Stanford. For fun, Larry still likes to invent things.

SERGEY BRIN

Sergey Mihailovich Brin, born in Moscow, Russia, in 1973, immigrated at the age of six with his family to the United States to escape the anti-Semitism Russia. In an October 28, 2000, interview, Sergey shared his thoughts on coming to the United States. He said that he was teased in school and didn't consider himself popular, but it didn't matter.

> I think, if anything, I feel like I have gotten a gift by being in the States rather than growing up in Russia. I know the hard times that my parents went through there, and I am very thankful that I was brought to the States. I think it just makes me appreciate my life much more.[2]

The family lived in Adelphi, Maryland, and his father, Michael Brin, was and still is a professor of mathematics at the University of Maryland. Sergey's mother, Eugenia, is a graduate of the School of Mechanics and Mathematics at Moscow State University. She is a scientist who works for NASA on projects related to climate and weather forecasting.

For his primary-grade schooling, Sergey, like Larry, attended a Montessori school. Like Larry, Sergey was filled with scientific curiosity as a youngster. He was interested in computers from an early age and received his first computer at age nine as a birthday present. After attending Eleanor Roosevelt High School, he started college in 1990 at the University of Maryland and graduated in three years with highest honors in mathematics and computer science.

With a graduate fellowship from the National Science Foundation, he started graduate school at Stanford, where he met Larry Page. He took a leave of absence to concentrate on Google after completing his master's degree in computer science.

In May 2007, Brin married Anne Wojcicki, a graduate of Yale University. Sergey is a gymnast and also likes to roller-blade and play sports during breaks at Google. He is president of technology at Google.

A Unique Wedding

Anne Wojcicki, a graduate of Yale, was a health care investment analyst before cofounding a biotech company called 23andMe, which offers individualized genetic mapping. Shortly after Sergey and Anne's wedding, Google disclosed in a regulatory filing that it had invested $3.9 million dollars in her start-up company.

Guests who attended the very secret wedding said that the bride and groom swam to a sandbar near a private Bermuda island to exchange vows. The bride wore a white bathing suit, and the groom wore a black bathing suit. The couple met when Google was still in its infancy. Anne's sister sublet Larry and Sergey space in her house for their first office.

When asked in an October 28, 2000, interview what he would like to be remembered for, Sergey answered that he'd like to be remembered for making the world a better place.

> One is through Google, the company, in terms of giving people access to information. I'm sure I will do other endeavors in terms of technologies and businesses. The second is just through philanthropy...I think that is the most important thing to me. I don't think my quality of life is really going to improve that much with more money.[3]

Now that we know a little bit about Larry and Sergey and how they met, we're ready to look more closely at what happened after they met.

NOTES

1. "Larry Page Interview," Academy of Achievement, October 28, 2000, http://www.achievement.org/autodoc/page/pag0int-1 (accessed January 21, 2008).
2. Ibid.
3. Ibid.

Chapter Two

The Origin and History of Google

Let's take a breezy, sky-high view of Google's history from before inception to the present. In the following chapters, we'll drill down into the revealing—and fascinating—details.

LARRY AND SERGEY MEET AGAIN

Larry and Sergey put the squabbling of their first meeting behind them after Larry started his graduate work at Stanford. He picked Dr. Terry Winograd as his advisor, who concentrated on the relatively new field of human-computer interaction (HCI).

Winograd led a project that received one of the first six awards made by the National Science Foundation in connection with the multiagency Digital Library Initiative in 1994. Larry received financial support from this award. He began to think about a project that could serve eventually as the basis for his dissertation. Winograd encouraged him to focus on the World Wide Web.

Larry and Sergey began to bond in their effort to solve a monumental problem in the World Wide Web environment: how can you find the best data for your purposes from an enormous amount of available data?

They soon found that that their different areas of expertise and shared interests served them well in their collaboration to solve this problem. Larry's strengths in invention and computer science made him a natural choice for taking on the challenge of cobbling together a bunch of low-end PCs to make a novel server environment that was not dependent on expensive high-end computers. Sergey was motivated by questions related to data mining, among others. He was also scouting around for a dissertation topic, and this area seemed like fertile ground for ideas. They named the new search engine they were creating BackRub because of its distinctive ability to analyze the "back links" pointing to a particular Web site. They developed a system of ranking the links that resulted from a search by relevance called PageRank.

Before long, Larry's dorm room was their first data center, packed with the PC network he had built. He and Sergey maxed out their credit cards to buy a terabyte of memory. Sergey created an office in his dorm room.

What Is a Terabyte?

Werner Buchholz coined the term *byte* in 1965. An octet, or eight bits, makes one byte. Bits are binary digits of ones or zeros. Eight bits make up the single byte that represents a single character, such as a single letter in a word. Over one trillion bytes make up a terabyte, which is more than eight trillion bits.

Computer systems need storage space for their operating systems, programs, files, and data.

Tera is the Greek word for *monster*. A terabyte is therefore a huge amount of hard disk drive storage area. So how much data can a terabyte store? Think about the more familiar megabyte. Slightly over one thousand megabytes equals one gigabyte, but just over one million megabytes equals a terabyte.

1,024 megabytes = 1 gigabyte
1,024 gigabytes = 1 terabyte
1,048,576 ($1,024^2$) megabytes = 1 terabyte

Consider that the average storage capacity of a home computer in the mid-1990s was 80 megabytes and that retail prices at that time were about one thousand dollars per four gigabytes. I think we can understand how Larry and Sergey maxed out their credit cards!

SEARCHING FOR PARTNERS

At this stage in their lives, Larry and Sergey weren't really interested in starting a company of their own. So they started shopping BackRub around to people who might want to partner with them. They wanted help to license a search technology that they believed beat the existing competition in its ability to retrieve the most relevant information on any given search topic.

They met with Yahoo! founder and friend David Filo, a Stanford graduate. He encouraged them to start their own search engine company but also told them to come back and talk to him when Google was fully developed. Other owners of established portal companies they talked to just weren't that interested. They didn't see that there was a market demand for a truly efficient search engine.

Larry and Sergey figured they were going to have to take a stand on their own. But to forge ahead with Google, they needed more space than their dorm rooms and they needed money to pay off their credit card debt. They created a business plan to show to potential investors.

MEETING WITH AN ANGEL

A friend of a faculty member and one of the founders of Sun Microsystems, Andy Bechtolsheim, was the first potential "angel" to whom they made their pitch and showed their demo.

Angel Investors

The term *angel investor* was originally used to describe the wealthy people who invested in Broadway plays. A business angel investor is an individual who often has enough business experience relevant to a company that he or she can understand a vision or a product in the early stages of a company's development in a way that other investors might not. Because of this ability to evaluate a company in its infancy, angels are willing to engage in high-risk investment and expect a high return on their investment. They sometimes provide expertise and contacts to the new company to help its growth.

Bechtolsheim was interested, he could see Google's potential, but he was pushed for time. Years later, Sergey recalls that early morning meeting:

We met him very early one morning on the porch of a Stanford faculty member's home in Palo Alto. We gave him a quick demo. He had to run off somewhere, so he said, "Instead of us discussing all the details, why don't I just write you a check?" It was made out to Google, Inc. and was for $100,000.[1]

Larry and Sergey must have been thrilled to find someone so respected in the world of computing who believed enough in Google to give them a check for $100,000. There was a problem, however. There was no corporation named Google, Inc. The check went into Larry's desk drawer for weeks while he and Sergey hustled to establish a legal corporation named Google, Inc. They also gathered more financial support from family and friends.

The domain *google.com* was registered on September 15, 1997. The company was incorporated on September 7, 1998.

GROWING PAINS

Google, Inc. found its first office space in Menlo Park, California. A friend sublet rooms to them that had a garage entrance. The space had perks in the form of a washer and dryer and a hot tub. Larry and Sergey also hired their first employee. Both the popular and industry press took notice, and the praise began. Google was named one of *PC Magazine*'s Top 100 Web Sites and Search Engines for 1998. Google was really taking off!

By 1999, search queries on Google had jumped from 10,000 per day to 500,000 per day. Staff size increased to eight, and the fledgling company moved into larger office space that sported a Ping-Pong table as boardroom furniture. They signed up their first commercial search customer. Just as important, they received an infusion of capital from leading venture capital firms for over $25 million. This was a huge vote of confidence.

What Is a Venture Capital Firm?

Venture capitalists provide money for companies just starting or for expansion. They want a high rate of return on their investment—as much as ten times the amount invested. They need such a good return from successful companies to make up for the companies they invest in that fail—the majority. Venture capitalists are professional investors who manage funds and look for promising investments for a fund. Unlike angel investors, venture capitalists might not have any expertise related to a particular company in which they want to invest.

MOVING TO THE GOOGLEPLEX

The company grew until it moved to what is called the Googleplex in Mountain View, California. Searches using Google jumped to 3 million a day after AOL/Netscape's selection of Google to provide its Web search service.

PC Magazine awarded Google its Technical Excellence Award for Innovation in Web Application Development. The company also made *Time* magazine's Top Ten Best Cybertech list for 1999.

What was life like in the year 2000 in the new Googleplex for the more than 60 employees working there? Well, there was open space rather than cubicles. Some employees brought their dogs to work. Modest desks consisted of wooden doors on sawhorses that supported powerful computers. Lava lamps were popular. Twice a week, the parking lot was converted to a roller hockey rink. Charlie Ayers, who had cooked for the Grateful Dead, came on board as chef.

Did any work get done in this unusual workplace that seemed, in some ways, like a big playground? Actually, the flexibility of the work space and "beyond casual" atmosphere nurtured collaboration. Gradual improvements were made to the search engine. The Google Directory was added. For users who needed or wanted to search in their native languages, the first 10 language versions were put in place. The quality of what Google had to offer and its ease of use increased the number of users beyond the wildest imagination—18 million user queries every day. Its popularity with a broad spectrum of humanity on the planet resulted in a Webby Award and a People's voice award for technical achievement in May 2000. Larry and Sergey delivered a five-word speech upon acceptance: "We love you, Google users!"

In June 2000, Google's introduction of its billion-page index officially made it the largest search engine in the world.

GROWING SUCCESS

The increase in users and awards weren't the only evidence of Google's success. New clients came on board to use Google as the search engine on their own sites. A keyword-targeted advertising program provided more revenue. Partnerships formed with Yahoo! and China's leading portal, among others. With the offering of innovative services to both large and small businesses, Google generated revenue and didn't need to seek additional money from investors at this stage.

And throughout 2000, it continued to offer enhancements to its users, including wireless search and Google Toolbar, both of which offered increased flexibility and ease of use.

Google acquired the archives of deja.com in 2001. Known as the Deja News Research Service in its early years, it was an archive of messages posted to Usenet discussion groups. (Usenet is a worldwide distributed Internet discussion system.) Google's powerful search engine enabled searches across all archived newsgroups. It also transformed Usenet from a loosely organized communication tool into an accessible information repository.

Google Groups was born from the deja.com archives with archive coverage extended back to 1981 and the addition of collections from private sources. It improved posting, post removal, and threading of the over 500 million messages exchanged over time on the Usenet discussion boards.

Did you ever wonder what topics other people in the world are searching? Introduced in 2001, Google Zeitgeist (www.google.com/press/zeitgeist.html) presents the most popular search trends with choices for year-end report, hot trends that shows the top searches for the past hour or less, and customized searches you can perform putting in your own keywords. The latter option invites you to satisfy your curiosity about the volume and pattern over time of a particular topic that could range from a product made by a company you're considering investing in to a vacation spot you're exploring for next winter. It also gives you the capability to compare the volume and pattern of several topics.

MAKING A PROFIT AND A NEW CEO

In the fourth quarter of 2001, Google was able to announce that it was making a profit. Dr. Eric Schmidt became Google's CEO, succeeding Larry

Page, the founding CEO. Larry's title changed to president, products. Schmidt came to Google with impressive leadership experience in strategic planning, management, and technology development from his time as CEO at Novell and chief technology officer and corporate executive officer at Sun Microsystems, Inc. Larry commented in a Google press release:

> Eric is exactly the right leader for Google....His extensive technology background and vision for the potential of the Internet complement the efforts that Google is making in defining a leadership position in Internet search and navigation. His strong management experience will help shape Google as we continue our growth and global expansion. And most importantly for anyone taking on the CEO role at Google, Eric is a natural fit with our corporate culture.[2]

Google's international presence continued to grow, as well, with new alliances in Asia and Latin America. Worldwide interest in Google advertising prompted opening additional sales offices in Hamburg and Tokyo.

As ever, Google's engineers worked constantly to improve the search engine. It learned some new tricks in 2001—it could crawl for new kinds of information based on file type such as image files. The Google Catalog Search (catalogs.google.com) made available for searching online more than 1,100 mail-order catalogs that before had been available only in print.

By the end of the year, Google's search index had grown to 3 billion searchable Web documents, moving Google further along the path toward its noble goal of making the world's information available online through search.

PROVIDING MORE SOLUTIONS AND NEW SERVICES

One of Google's strengths is identifying a variety of challenges or needs and trying to provide solutions to the diverse audience of Google users. It also identifies and anticipates needs very well and provides services to meet them.

In 2002, Google solved the problem of how to enable corporations' and other organizations' sites that were secured behind firewalls to use Google as their search engine behind those firewalls. Prior to this time, Googlebot, the robot software that crawls the Web to increase the number of documents available to searchers and to update already indexed documents, couldn't go past firewalls to be used as an in-house search engine to search through a firewalled organization's own documents.

The Google Search Appliance, also called "Google in a box," was the plug-and-play solution that allowed organizations to use the Google search engine to search their own collections of documents that they wished to keep secure from the rest of the world.

To increase its reach and to find solutions to technical challenges, Google encourages dialogue with programmers and techies outside the Googleplex. Two of the ways it did this in 2002 were through Google Labs (labs.google.com) and the Google Programming Contest (www.google. com/programming-contest).

The introduction of Google Labs on the Google Web site gave Google engineers a chance to show off some of their new ideas as they were developing them. They welcomed constructive feedback on their "babies" from interested viewers and programmers from all over the world.

Google offered a Google Programming Contest in 2002 that gave contestants 900,000 raw Web pages and challenged them to write a program that would do something interesting with the data. The winner would receive $10,000 in cash, a visit to the Googleplex, and, if possible, a running of their code on Google's document repository. (For more, see www. google.com/programming-contest/winner.html.)

The free service Google News (news.google.com) launched in beta form in September 2002. It offered users one place to search and browse through over 4,000 worldwide news sources. What a great resource when you need to crank out a paper quickly for a social studies class!

And, for those too busy to run around town to find just the perfect CD player? Google started testing Froogle (later named Google Product Search—www.google.com/products), which helps users find many sources for specific products and offers pictures and prices of what they want to buy.

MORE RECOGNITION

The year 2002 brought more awards and high praise. Webmasters selected Google for their highest honors of its 2001 Search Engine Watch Awards, including Outstanding Search Service, Best Image Search Engine, Best Design, Most Webmaster Friendly Search Engine, and Best Search Feature.

America Online called Google "the reigning champ of online search." It selected the company to provide both search capability and advertising to AOL's 34 million members and its tens of millions visitors. *BtoB Magazine* named Google the top business-to-business Web site.

BLOGS AND MORE

Google added Blogger (www.blogger.com/start), a way to create online journals, to its site in 2003. It also added the Google AdSense program based on a technology that evaluates text on a page and then creates meaningful advertisements (www.google.com/adsense). This program had the potential to bring benefits to Web sites large and small. Google Deskbar was a new release located in the Windows Taskbar that enabled the user to access Google without opening a browser.

THE SKY'S THE LIMIT

After Google's site index reached 4.28 billion Web pages and Brand-channel named Google as Brand of the Year for 2003, Larry and Sergey were named Persons of the Week by ABC News. The site index total jumped to 6 billion items before the year was out and 800 million images. Local search was a handy new service that helped people find products and services within their localities.

Google, with good humor, made one of its most exciting announcements on April 1, 2004. It plans to open a research facility on the moon called Google Copernicus Hosting Environment and Experiment in Search Engineering (G.C.H.E.E.S.E.). One of the possible outcomes of this research facility will be the ability to record every radio and television signal broadcast from earth with the idea of making them available to anyone with a computer.

> With the establishment of the Copernicus Center, Google's mission has grown beyond "organizing the world's information and making it universally accessible and useful." Our new goal is to "organize all the useful information in the universe and serve it to you on a lightly salted cracker."[3]

As it turns out, this announcement on the Web site was an April Fool's Day prank.

Other new services besides local search were Google Gmail (www.mail.google.com) and Google Desktop Search (desktop.google.com). Gmail, a Web-based mail service, was launched offering users enough storage space to save years' of messages. Google Desktop search is a free downloadable program to help people find files on their own computers.

With the addition of Google Earth (earth.google.com), Google users gained the ability to search digital and satellite image maps and enjoy the thrill of a flight simulator as they explored. High-resolution three-dimensional images enhance virtual tours of cities and countryside. Space travel to see galaxies and planets is at the Google Earth user's fingertips as well.

In August 2004, Google offered shares of the company for sale to the public through an auction process intended to attract a broad range of investors. The first quarterly results as a public company showed revenues of over $800 million.

Google continued to expand its international footprint with the opening of a new headquarters in Dublin and a research and development center in Tokyo in 2004. The following year, it opened a new sales office in Stockholm, Sweden, and a research and development center in China. The first offices in Latin America opened as well.

Larry and Sergey continued to receive accolades. Larry was inducted into the National Academy of Engineering. Both he and Sergey were named the 2004 Marconi Fellows.

BOOKS, MUSIC, AND MORE COMMUNICATION TOOLS

Larry and Sergey announced Google Print (books.google.com) in fall 2004 at the Frankfurt Book Fair in Germany. Highly respected publishers such as Cambridge University Press, Blackwell, and Oxford University Press were some of the first to join the program. Harvard, Stanford, the University of Michigan, the University of Oxford, and the New York Public Library agreed to scan books from their collections to participate in the Google Print program. Two years later, the University of California, the University of Wisconsin, and the University of Virginia agreed to partner with Google to digitize and make searchable millions of pages of documents in their libraries.

A new music search tool that provides information on musicians and performers as well as links to albums was offered near the end of 2005. Google offered this as a rather subtle service within search. After typing in the name of a popular group in the Google search box—like the Beach Boys—Google will return information about the group or artist including reviews, links to where you can buy CDs or downloads, and sometimes images of album covers. Google hopes to expand this program over time by adding classical musicians, more groups and individual musicians from other countries and lesser-known performers—not just musicians popular in the United States.

Google Talk (www.google.com/talk/) gave PC users a free way to speak to each other via computer as well as voice mail and instant messaging. The acquisition of JotSpot, a prominent wiki platform, promises groups a way to collaborate for enhanced productivity.

FOR VIDEO AND FILM BUFFS

The year 2006 brought many new features to video and film buffs with Google video store and the Google Video Player. Google also started a pilot program with the National Archives in Washington, D.C. (www.google.com/intl/en/press/pressrel/video_nara.html), digitizing and making available historical film footage. (For an index of films, head to http://video.google.com/nara.html.)

Google Video was launched in local languages in Canada, France, Germany, Italy, The Netherlands, Poland, Spain, and the United Kingdom. In October 2006, Google acquired the popular YouTube.

NOT ONLY NOT DOING EVIL, BUT DOING GOOD

Google has served humanity well by making incredible amounts of information available to the segment of the world's population that has access to computers. Sergey's motto for Google—"Don't be evil"— morphed into actively doing good around specific causes with the advent of Google.org.

Google is focused on the three global challenges of climate change, poverty, and emerging disease. It hopes to use its resources and partnerships with these initiatives for:

- The development of renewable energy that is less expensive than coal.
- The promotion of the commercialization of plug-in vehicles.
- The anticipation and prevention of threats such as disease and climate risk.
- The provision of information to empower efforts to improve public services such as health, education, water, and sanitation.
- The support of the growth of small and medium-sized enterprises in the developing world.

Google is serious about trying to be a good corporate citizen. The company recycles as much as possible, it supports hybrid technologies, encourages its employees to use car pools and shuttles, and installed a large solar panel at their Mountain View Googleplex. The solar panel is one of the largest on any corporate site in the world and it is the largest in the United States.

A HUGE LEAP IN LESS THAN 10 YEARS

Obviously, Larry and Sergey made incredible progress in less than a decade building Google. The last quarter of 2006, Google reported revenues of $3.21 billion and a net income of $1.03 billion just for that quarter. It employs over 10,000 people around the world. Search results are now available in more than 35 languages, and Google has an audience of over 380 million people worldwide.

This history of their incredible growth and productivity covers some of the highlights of the partnerships, acquisitions, products, and services that happened during this time. These are just some of the surface events that describe Google's brief history. Naturally, there's a lot more to the story, which we'll investigate in the coming chapters. But some important trends emerge from these highlights: Google is committed to innovation and to the ongoing improvement of existing services and products. It listens to its users to continue to develop what they need and want. It forms partnerships with an array of businesses and institutions to bring information and enhanced services and products to its audience. Finally, Google attempts to tread as lightly on the earth as a corporate giant can, and it is starting to apply capital and expertise to worldwide problems.

NOTES

1. "Google Milestones," Google Corporate Information, http://www.google.com/corporate/history.html (accessed January 27, 2008).

2. "Google Names Dr. Eric Schmidt Chief Executive Officer," Google Press Center, August 6, 2001, http://www.google.com/press/pressrel/ceo.html (accessed January 27, 2008).

3. "Why a Lunar Location?" Google Job Opportunities, http://www.google.com/intl/en/jobs/lunar_job2.html (accessed January 27, 2008).

Chapter Three

Internet Search: The Historical Context

All companies are products, to some degree, of the historical contexts into which they are born. Google couldn't happen without the technological advances that preceded it. But what makes it better than the competition is what it created that moved the company beyond the rest of the pack, beyond what had been accomplished to that point.

Without the existence of the Internet and the World Wide Web, Google might have been conceived of as an idea, but there would not have been any collection of information for it to search, index, and make available to the world. We can better understand Google if we step back in time to consider how the Internet and the Web came to be and what attempts were made to search and organize the information that grew so quickly on the Web before Google was born.

The first historical event we'll consider took place in 1957—sixteen years before Larry Page and Sergey Brin were born.

RESPONDING TO THE POSSIBILITY OF NUCLEAR WAR

Dwight D. Eisenhower was president of the United States in 1957, the year that the USSR launched *Sputnik,* the first artificial earth satellite. In response, the United States created the Advanced Research Projects Agency (ARPA) as part of the Department of Defense. The purpose of ARPA was to enable the United States to compete with the Soviet Union for leadership in technology related to the military. ARPA assembled some of the most brilliant minds in the country, and, in eighteen months, the United States successfully launched its own satellite.

The U.S. government at the time was concerned about the possible loss of mobility and communication during a nuclear war. The Dwight D. Eisenhower National System of Interstate and Defense Highways— more commonly called the Interstate Highway system and the same ones most of us drive on frequently—was approved in response to the fear of loss of mobility. In response to the fear of loss of communication, ARPA, over the next few years, under the direction of Dr. J.C.R. Licklider, would

USSR

USSR stands for the Union of Soviet Socialist Republics and was also known as Russia and the Soviet Union. It was established in 1922 and included Russia and 14 other Soviet socialist republics. The United States and the USSR were engaged in what was known as the Cold War between 1945 and the dissolution of the Soviet Union in 1991. The so-called space race, which initially was concerned with who would launch the first satellite, was part of the Cold War, as was a huge arms buildup on both sides. Although it is hard to imagine now, the Soviet Union and the United States were the two superpowers on the planet, and their adversarial relationship influenced everything from foreign affairs and military operations to culture and global economics worldwide.

---

concentrate on research designed to improve the military's use of computers. In 1962, Licklider wrote a visionary paper about a galactic network of globally interconnected computers.

The design for the Advanced Research Projects Agency Network (ARPANET) was completed in 1966. In 1969, the first message was sent by what we now call the Internet from a computer node at the University of California to a second node at Stanford Research Institute. The project had succeeded in creating an alternative method of communication to the telephone. It would eventually be able to reach any corner of the world that had a computer and a telephone or other network access. Could the new system, and its present-day version, survive a nuclear attack? We all hope it's never tested in that way, but some experts speculate that the electromagnetic pulse that would result from a nuclear explosion would cripple all electronics.

EARLY INTERNET SEARCH ENGINES
WITH COMIC BOOK NAMES

In 1990, Alan Emtage, a student at Montreal's McGill University, created Archie (an abbreviation for archives), the first program that could download the directory listings of public files on the Internet and create a searchable database of them. It wasn't the least bit user friendly because you had to know Unix commands to use it, and it took considerable knowledge of this computer language to use Archie fully. Nevertheless, the demand for this kind of tool was so great and traffic was so heavy on Archie that McGill decided to deny anyone outside the university access to it. Fortunately, by then other early Internet search engines were becoming available.

Gopher, named after the University of Minnesota's mascot by its creator Mark McCahill in 1991, indexed plain text documents. Jughead and Veronica soon followed, and they searched file names and titles stored in Gopher index systems. Veronica was better than Archie in some ways. Veronica was more frequently updated and it could be searched directly from most of the big Gopher menus. Veronica indexed the full title of a document instead of just the file name, making it easier to find documents. It also connected someone searching for a document directly to the file with a single click.

The Wide Area Information Server (WAIS) fully indexed all the text in Gopher and other Internet documents. In this sense, it was a significant forerunner to modern search engines. It was developed in 1991 by Brewster Kahle at Xerox PARC. WAIS's glory was genuine but short lived when it was eclipsed by the surging growth of the World Wide Web. Archie, Veronica, Jughead, and Gopher met the same fate.

Xerox PARC

Xerox PARC was a pioneer in technology that would become standard for much of the computing industry. Now known as PARC (Palo Alto Research Center, Inc.), it started out as a division of Xerox Corporation in 1970. In 2002, it became a wholly owned subsidiary of Xerox. In the early 1970s, its Alto personal computer demonstrated the use of the world's first what-you-see-is-what-you-get (WYSIWYG) editor, a commercial mouse for input, and a graphical user interface including menus and icons that would influence the development of both Windows and Macintosh interfaces. PARC continues to be a leading source of innovation for technology-driven industries. For example, in partnership with SolFocus, Inc., it has developed a highly efficient low-cost solar concentrator for solar panels as part of its Cleantech Innovation Program (www.parc.com/research/projects/cleantech/de fault.html).

Even though these early methods of information storage and retrieval were primitive by today's standards, the amount of information being put on the Internet grew rapidly. The need for an easier way to share it and access it increased rapidly right along with the growth of information.

THE WORLD WIDE WEB

At the time Larry and Sergey developed the Google search engine in 1998, the World Wide Web had been in existence for only about five years. Tim Berners-Lee, an independent English contractor working at CERN, the European Particle Physics Laboratory, built a prototype of the Web in

1980 called Enquire. Berners-Lee was attempting to develop a system that would make it easier for researchers, scientists, and other academics to share information.

He returned to CERN as a fellow in 1984. CERN was the largest Internet node in Europe in 1989, and Berners-Lee started thinking about his earlier project Enquire.

CERN, like other large organizations, had information scattered on many different computers. The people at CERN came from many different universities all over the world. They used different types of computers and different types of computer software programs. It was a challenge to try to share information. Berners-Lee wrote many computer programs so that information could be shared from one type of computer to another. Finally, he decided he wanted to solve this problem once and for all. A colleague at CERN, Robert Cailliau, collaborated on getting funding for the project. Berners-Lee renewed the work he started with Enquire using hypertext markup language (HTML) in connection with the Internet.

Hypertext is a term coined by an engineer named Ted Nelson around 1965. Hypertext is a way to create text with hot links that you can click on, as you know, to go to other documents or images. The Internet is a huge worldwide network of computers that communicate with each other using certain protocols such as the Transmission Control Protocol (TCP) and the Internet Protocol (IP).

Berners-Lee created the first Web browser and Web editor called the WorldWideWeb. (Later, it would be spelled with spaces between the words.) The Web browser and Web editor were computer programs that could interpret hypertext documents. It formatted them into Web pages in a version that could be viewed by the user.

Berners-Lee's system allowed everyone to share and access information no matter what kind of computer they were using, no matter what operating system they were using, and no matter what Web browser they were running on their computers. Also, since the information (a file) was only being read (never written) by a Web browser, it was possible for multiple users to be reading the same information (file) at the same time.

Berners-Lee created the first Web site and put it online in August 1991. The Web site explained what the World Wide Web was and how to set up a Web server. Later, he created the world's first Web directory based on a list of other Web sites that he collected. He eventually created the Virtual Library, the oldest catalog of the Web. In 1993, CERN's directors issued a declaration that the World Wide Web technology would be free to anyone to use.

THE EARLY YEARS OF SEARCHING THE WORLD WIDE WEB

In three short years, from 1993 to 1996, the number of Web sites grew from 130 to more than 600,000. The Web grew faster than mere humans could track. The challenge now for researchers was to figure out what information was on the Web and how people searching for information could find what they needed.

In June 1993, a researcher at the Massachusetts Institute of Technology named Matthew Gray developed the first Web-based search engine. His World Wide Wanderer tracked the growth of the Web and created an index of sites. Gray created a search interface that made it possible for people search the index.

Search Engines

Search engines make it possible for us to find the information we want on the World Wide Web.

Three computer programs coordinate to make a search engine work. The first program is called a spider (sometimes referred to as a crawler or a bot). It reads (crawls) the pages on Web sites, including the hypertext links on each page. The second program creates a comprehensive index or catalog of the pages that the spider has read. The third program processes your search terms or what you ask it to search for, looks for it in the index, and returns a list of possible sites for you to consider.

Meta search engines offer the user search results from other search engines after reranking those results. In the early days, when each search engine had a unique index because of variations in how they crawled the web and there were variations in how efficient some engines were, this was a valuable service. It helped to ensure that Web sites relevant to your search didn't slip through the gaps. As search technology has improved, the need for meta search engines, like dog pile.com, has decreased.

Vertical search engines are specialized. They look for information in a narrowly defined area of interest. For example, SearchGov.com is a search engine that crawls U.S. government and state government Web sites. MedlinePlus offers medical information from the U.S. National Library of Medicine and the U.S. National Institutes of Health. NexTag offers comparison shopping with user ratings and prices that include tax and shipping charges. TripAdvisor.com helps users find reviews and information about travel destinations and lodging.

Three bot-fed search engines emerged six months later. They were JumpStation, the World Wide Web Worm, and Repository-Based Software Engineering (RBSE) spider. The first two search engines offered the searcher a list of results in the order in which they were found without concern for quality. RBSE did have a ranking system. The concept of a ranking system attempted to solve another problem: When searching the

Web, how can you find the highest quality or most relevant information? This would be a challenge that Larry and Sergey would take on.

Bots

Computer robots, or bots, are computer programs that automate repetitive tasks at speeds impossible for humans to reproduce.

Let's take a look at a sample of the search engines that existed before Google. We'll get a sense of what had been accomplished in the development of search engine capabilities before Larry and Sergey stepped up to the plate.

EXCITE

Six Stanford undergraduate students launched Excite in 1993. In an effort to make searching more efficient, they used statistical analysis of word relationships. After they were funded, they made copies of their search software available for use on Web sites. Excite was the first company to give users the ability to create personalized Web pages with news, regional weather reports, and business information through MyExcite. They were the first major player to offer free e-mail.

LYCOS, ALTA VISTA, AND WEBCRAWLER

On the heels of Excite's success, 1994 was a banner year for the emergence of new search engines. Lycos, Alta Vista, Web Crawler, and Infoseek were made available to the public that year.

Lycos

Designed at Carnegie Mellon University by Dr. Michael Mauldin, Lycos was one of the first search engines to use links to a page to determine how relevant a page was. This would later be a key feature of Google's PageRank system for determining relevance. It also used more refined algorithms to analyze a Web page's meaning. Another significant difference between Lycos and other search engines was the size of its catalog. It offered users a summary of what was on a Web page instead of just a list of links. In fall 1994, it ranked as number one on Netscape's list of search engines. Lycos, by 1996, had more documents in its index than any other search engine crawling the Web.

Alta Vista

The number of Web pages and links on them to other Web pages was growing at an incredibly fast pace. A single Web crawler that trundled along in a straight line storing and indexing each page and link would never be able to complete the job before the Web had grown and changed significantly. Digital Equipment Corporation had developed a computer system that was powerful enough to send a thousand crawlers out on the Web at the same time. The result was the most complete index of the Web at the time.

Alta Vista was the first to offer users the ability to put in search terms in natural language. It also offered advanced search features and search tips.

WebCrawler

Brian Pinkerton, a computer science and engineering student at the University of Washington, made WebCrawler available to the public in 1994. It was the first search engine that could index entire Web pages. It had a database comprised of pages from slightly over 4,000 different Web sites. It was so popular, with traffic on the site so heavy during daytime hours, that it was almost impossible to get on the site. Seven months after it became available, WebCrawler responded to its one millionth query. By fall 1995, WebCrawler was fully funded by advertising that it sold. It maintained the integrity of its search results by separating the advertising from the search results. In June 1995, America Online purchased Web-Crawler and ran it on its network, because, at that time, it did not have its own Web search capability to offer to members.

WebCrawler set the standard for all major search engines that came after it by letting its users search for any word in any web page. It was also the first search engine to really catch on with the public and to gain a wide following. In April 1996, WebCrawler, in addition to pure search, added a human-edited guide for the Web called GNN Select, which had previously been known as the Whole Internet Catalog.

In 1997, WebCrawler was sold to Excite.

THE LIBRARIANS' INDEX TO THE INTERNET (LII)

Carole Leita was a reference librarian at the Berkeley Public Library from 1978 to 1997. The Librarians' Index to the Internet came into the world as Carole's Gopher bookmark file in 1991. Her file was composed of useful sites that librarians would likely want to return to repeatedly as they helped library patrons in their searches for information. It was called the Berkeley Public Library Index to the Internet from 1994 to 1996, when it first became a Web site.

Carole and Roy Tennant at the University of California, Berkeley's Digital Library SunSITE worked to add a search engine and a content management system to the index starting in 1996. The index was moved to the UC Berkeley SunSITE in 1997 and renamed the Librarians' Index to the Internet (LII). That same year, the project received funding from the Library Services and Technology Act. The funding supported recruiting and training volunteer contributors to the index as well as more editorial support. The site caught on like wildfire with librarians and the public worldwide. The project now includes a weekly newsletter with 40,000 subscribers.

What was so remarkable about this index? Why has it become so trusted and so popular? Péter Jacsó's review entitled "Librarians' Index to the Internet" in the March 2001 *Digital Reference Review* offers clear answers to these questions:

> There are thousands of subject guides and directories of Web resources. Those who have not yet created one are likely to be working on one. *LII* stands out from the crowd thanks to its professionalism, objectivity, reasonable selection policy, informative annotations, excellent organization, awesome interface and search features.[1]

In 2005, the name of the index was shortened to Librarians' Internet Index.

Until October 2001, when she retired from full-time work, Carole was the coordinator of the LII Web site. She answered some questions for me about search before and after Google.

VS: Why did you start the LII?

CL: I wanted to index interesting and useful stuff that librarians would want to get to.

VS: As a reference librarian who was responsible for finding information library patrons needed, how would you characterize the search process before the advent of the World Wide Web?

CL: Before the World Wide Web, most search was paper based. You'd have to decide where to start depending on the question, the background of the questioner, and the use to which they would put the information. Everything was dependent on understanding the question and that determined which paper-based index a librarian selected initially. There was no universal place to begin searching.

VS: Once Google was available, did the process of searching for information change radically?

CL: People are shy about sharing what they're looking for and why and so if they can look it up themselves they're happier. Search on Google can be more efficient. The process of where to go as a first place to search has changed since Google. That is the major change. It's an index that collects so much information and ranks it in a way that is so successful.

VS: Do reference librarians rely on Google more than other search engines?

CL: Yes, most librarians will start their search there if they haven't identified (from the reference interview) an easily available database or paper source.

VS: What made Google different from search engines before it?

CL: Google is faster, more comprehensive, and more efficient in sorting the better information to the top of the results list. It has a simple design with an obvious search box. Without the clutter of all the advertising and portal sections of its competitors it's easier to use.

VS: How did Google change search for the average person without any specialized skills in search?

CL: Google's PageRank system, by putting the most important information first, supports a user who may not have enough background knowledge to evaluate the quality of the choices given by other search engines.

VS: Besides its search capability, what other features of Google do you consider to be of value?

CL: All of them [laughing]. See http://www.google.com/intl/en/ options. Really important for work is the software for collaborative work on documents on the Net—Google Docs.

VS: Are there special tools or features that Google has to offer that you enjoy using?

CL: Google Alerts is something I like. I set up a search on a topic or person I want to follow and I'm emailed an alert with a link to my topic whenever something new shows up in Google's index.

How Is a Directory Different from a Search Engine?

Most modern search engines have some kind of editorial review process that's done by people. But the relevancy or quality of Web pages relative to a search word(s) is mostly determined by automated search algorithms such as Google's PageRank. Directories are not automated like search engines. They require people to review Web sites to judge their quality and to return to those sites to review them as the sites change. As you might imagine, this process takes a lot of time and costs more than using an automated search engine to do this job unless volunteers create the index.

YAHOO!

David Filo and Jerry Yang were electrical engineering doctoral students at Stanford University in 1994. As you may recall, David Filo encouraged Larry and Sergey to continue their work on Google when they were just getting started, looking for funding and partners before they finally started their own company.

Yahoo! started out as a list of Jerry and David's favorite links to Internet sites that had information on topics that interested them. When their lists got too long, they created categories of topics. When the information in categories got too big, they created subcategories. The heart of the Yahoo! approach to the World Wide Web—a directory of information—was born. Although there were others who created Web directories, theirs became the most popular and is still popular today.

Their Web site initially was called Jerry and David's Guide to the World Wide Web. They later found a new name for their site in a dictionary. They liked the definition for the word *yahoo:* "rude, unsophisticated, and uncouth." They later added the exclamation point to the name to avoid conflict with other existing products that were using Yahoo already.

Jerry and David created a guide to useful Web sites that turned out to be very appealing to others looking for specific information on the Web. Just their friends used it at first, but, before long, word spread until they had enthusiastic users from the larger Internet community. By fall 1994, around 100,000 visitors had used the directory.

Jerry and David knew they had created a potential winner. They tried to sell their creation, but nobody was buying. By March 1995, the pair incorporated Yahoo! and started looking for venture capital. They connected with highly respected Sequoia Capital, which had funded companies like Cisco, Apple Computer, Oracle, and Atari. Sequoia invested close to $2 million. Anticipating explosive growth, the founders started putting together their management team. They received a second round of funding from Reuters Ltd and Softbank in the fall of 1995. In late 1995, they started generating revenue with banner ads. The previous year, a Web content portal called Hotwired had started the practice and Yahoo! followed suit.

A Different Kind of Directory—The Open Directory Project

The Open Directory Project was different from the Yahoo! directory in that its content was created and almost entirely maintained by a group of volunteer editors. Over time, it became the largest directory on the Web. It had indexed over 4 million Web addresses by 2003. By March 2007, over 75,000 volunteer editors had contributed to the project. The Open Directory Project was purchased by Netscape in 1998. Netscape soon was acquired by America Online, which later merged with Time Warner. The Open Directory Project claims to be "the largest, most comprehensive human-edited directory" (www.dmoz.org) of the Web, with 79,869 editors and over 590,000 categories of information.

Yahoo!'s initial public offering (IPO) of stock came in April 1996. The company, by then, had grown to 49 employees.

Yahoo! has a history of making deals with other companies to use their search engines to power their own search service. Inktomi provided those services by 2001. Yahoo! acquired Inktomi and Overture in 2003. It used Google's search engine until 2004 while it was getting into a position to use its own search engine based on the technology of the companies it had acquired.

Although it has felt the impact of Google on its market in recent years, Yahoo has been a hugely successful company providing services to more than 345 million people each month. It has offices in Canada, Australia, Latin America, Europe, Asia, and other parts of the United States besides its Sunnyvale, California, headquarters. In February 2008, Microsoft, as part of its strategy to better compete with Google, made a hostile bid for Yahoo! of $42 billion that Yahoo!, as of this writing, turned down.

INKTOMI

University of California, Berkeley professor Eric Brewer and Paul Gauthier, a graduate student, founded the Inktomi Corporation in 1995. They developed software that was used in the HotBot search engine. Hot-Bot surpassed Alta Vista as the leading Web-crawler search engine. Inktomi solved some technical issues related to the scale of search by using a distributed network technology—many computers—versus Alta Vista's single powerful Alpha processor. Inktomi claimed that it refined the quality of search by trying to convert human analysis to a process of computerized analysis of links to find the most popular and productive Web sites on a given subject. But it failed to develop a successful business model and, as mentioned, Yahoo! acquired Inktomi in 2003.

ASK.COM (FORMERLY ASK JEEVES)

Ask Jeeves was a unique search service that was launched in April 1997 through the combined efforts of venture capitalist Garrett Gruener and technologist David Warthen. The name of the service was based on the character Jeeves, the valet in the well-known novels and short stories of English writer P. G. Wodehouse. The idea then, behind the Web site's name and its format, was to put the brilliant and charming Jeeves at people's disposal when they had a question that they couldn't answer themselves.

Jeeves was a natural language search engine, which meant you could ask it a question as though you were speaking to another person. Ask Jeeves used a staff to build a huge database of questions that they anticipated users would ask. Then, they chose Web pages that provided answers to this database of questions. In this manner, Ask Jeeves provided searchers with a search experience that simulated interaction with another human—in this case, the lovable and reliable Jeeves.

Ask Jeeves used editors who tried to match search queries, and it used the search engine called DirectHit that tried to rank results based on their popularity. Ask Jeeves caught the public's attention quickly, becoming a top-25 Web destination by early 2000. By 2006, the Jeeves character was phased out and the site became simply Ask.com.

MSN SEARCH

In 1998, Microsoft introduced its search service based on results from Inktomi. It blended in results from Looksmart, another search engine, shortly thereafter. It also briefly used results from Alta Vista. In 2004, Microsoft began to switch over to its own search technology backed by its own Web crawler, msnbot. Microsoft changed the name of its search to Live Search, which became available to the public in its final form in September 2006.

WAS THERE ROOM FOR ANOTHER SEARCH ENGINE?

Given the number of search engines that were popping up like mushrooms on a moist forest floor in spring, it seems like a fair question to ask whether there was room for yet another one. It might also be fair to ask whether the search process could be improved. Let's do a quick review of what we learned about what various search engines had been able to accomplish before Google. After all, even as early as 1991, before the Web was born, the WAIS had demonstrated that a full-text index of a vast array of documents could be produced.

In answer to the relevancy challenge, RBSE had developed a system of ranking Web pages in 1993 as an early attempt to help searchers find relevant information to their queries. In the same year, Excite contributed statistical analysis of word relationships to increase efficiency in searching. Lycos's Mauldin was one of the first to use links to a page to evaluate how relevant a page was to a particular search. Pinkerton's WebCrawler proved that a search engine could be developed that could index entire Web pages including the HTML coding that made it a Web page and not just titles. Alta Vista demonstrated that, with a powerful enough system, a nearly complete index of Web pages could be generated. When the Web grew and that task seemed more daunting—even when using a system as powerful as Alta Vista's that could support a thousand crawlers at one time—HotBot offered the answer to the scale problem by using distributed network technology. On the user's side of the search engine, the search process had become easier when search terms could be put in natural language and online search tips provided support.

Yahoo! created an extremely popular Web portal with its directories even if it didn't do its own search. It offered a new way of organizing the information on the Web into categories and subcategories. In April 1996, after receiving two rounds of venture capital, it raised over $30 million with its initial public offering. Given its popularity with users, the attention it received from the press, the vision and energy of its founders, and the capital it raised from its IPO, Yahoo! was well positioned to become a leader in the industry.

Lycos had grown rapidly, and by 1999 it was the most visited online destination in the world. In retrospect, we can understand how valuable it was—it sold for $5.4 billion in 2000. MSN, of course, had the brand name and capital of Microsoft behind it when it came on the scene in 1998, which made it a formidable potential force.

Given this scenario of these three strong contenders, not to mention many other established search engines, was there room for Google? Was there a need for Google? A comment of Joe Krause, cofounder of Excite, helps us answer this question as he reflects on the state of the search industry in the mid-1990s: "All the portals suffered from the classic business mistake of veering from their core mission. Unbeknownst to them all, there was a giant vacuum left in search."[2]

The giant vacuum was not unbeknownst to Larry and Sergey. They published a paper while they were still graduate students at Stanford in which they presented Google as a prototype. In "The Anatomy of a Large-Scale Hypertextual Web Search Engine," they wrote, "Google is designed to crawl and index the Web efficiently and produce much more satisfying search results than existing systems."[3]

In upcoming chapters, we'll look more closely at what made Google more efficient and able to "produce much more satisfying search results than existing systems." We'll also explore what else Larry and Sergey created through Google that made them so successful and made the world a different place for those with access to Google.

NOTES

1. http://www.galegroup.com/servlet/HTMLFileServlet?imprint=9999&re gion=7&fileName=reference/archive/200103/lii.html (accessed February 1, 2008).

2. John Battelle, *The Search: How Google and Its Rivals Rewrote the Rules of Business and Transformed Our Culture* (New York: Penguin Group, 2005), p. 57.

3. Sergey Brin and Lawrence Page, "The Anatomy of a Large-Scale Hypertextual Web Search Engine," Stanford University InfoLab, http://infolab.stanford.edu/~backrub/google.html (accessed February 10, 2008).

Chapter Four

What Made Google So Much Better?

At this point in the history of search, 2008, Google is the undisputed king. It's the site most visited by users from all over the world who want to find information. But at the time Larry and Sergey made their claim that "Google is designed to crawl and index the Web efficiently and produce much more satisfying search results than existing systems," Google was not yet the number one destination for search. In this chapter, we'll consider what made Google better than the competition. We'll also see how Google parlayed its excellent search engine into a money-making machine.

Google's success began and it continues because of its intense commitment to providing users with the most relevant search results. On Google's corporate information Web page, under the heading of "Ten things Google has found to be true," we're told:

> It's best to do one thing really, really well.
> Google does search. With one of the world's largest research groups focused exclusively on solving search problems, we know what we do well, and how we could do it better....As we continue to build new products while making search better, our hope is to bring the power of search to previously unexplored areas, and to help users access and use even more of the ever-expanding information in their lives."[1]

This intense focus on the quality of search results has helped ensure that Google has, in its own words, "built the most loyal audience on the web."[2]

Over a relatively short period of time, Larry and Sergey built a company that became wildly successful. In this chapter, we'll look at how Google became the best company in its industry by:

- building a search engine that rapidly returned the best search results
- attracting venture capital to finance early growth

- building an infrastructure—a computer network—to support growth that eventually would be so huge that it serves as a barrier to new entrants into the field of search who might challenge the company
- creating a business strategy based on its core competency of excellent search results that generated revenue from alliances, partnerships, and acquisitions
- generating revenue from ads tied to search without compromising the integrity of the search
- diversifying its products within the context of its mission of making all the information in the world available to everyone by concentrating on what Google users need to better receive, manipulate, customize, communicate, and use the specific information they need and in a variety of media
- establishing strong ongoing global relationships with businesses that use its products and services and individuals who use search
- creating a corporate structure and corporate culture that was designed to let Google control its destiny and to attract and keep the most brilliant team of engineers in the universe of search.

The timing of Larry and Sergey's development of the Google search engine was lucky. They had the benefit of looking objectively at the positive and negative attributes of search engines already in use. Once venture capital supported them, they had the time and the funding to continue improving the search engine, develop a brilliant and dedicated team, build an infrastructure, and develop sources of revenue.

THE CAPTIVATING CHALLENGES

It's important to consider the frame of mind Larry and Sergey were in, as graduate students, when they were developing Google. They were captivated by the challenges inherent in developing the best search engine in the world. In this sense, it was a pure quest and, in many significant ways, it has remained a pure quest that continues to inspire them and the people who work for them and to serve as the underpinning of everything they do with Google.

In the course of their research at Stanford, they were well aware of the challenges of creating a perfect search engine that could rapidly search and index all of the information on the Web, which was already huge and growing constantly. The number of people searching for information was growing dramatically. Other search engines had been able to meet these challenges to some extent. What had not been done well up to this point, partly because no one was really interested in the problem, was to devise a way to find and present the most *relevant* information in response to a search query. Many companies were selling top search results, and not all companies identified them as paid results.

Searching and finding relevant results was becoming more difficult and tedious. Searchers had to bushwhack through jungles of blatant advertising that cluttered the page. The first results returned to them, supposedly the most relevant, were paid for by advertisers and were not necessarily relevant or the best. To make matters worse, search results had become tainted by spammers.

Spam

Surely all of us who have spent time on a computer have experienced being spammed. Spam is junk mail and advertising sent to us along with who knows how many people by someone who wants to sell us something. It is unwanted advertising that usually has nothing to do with our search terms. The effect is somewhat like a bandit showing up in our lives, stealing our time and attention.

Larry and Sergey also knew what had already been accomplished in the realm of search. They knew the capabilities of other search engines. After looking at the challenges and the accomplishments, they claimed, in a paper titled "The Anatomy of a Large-Scale Hypertextual Web Search Engine," that "Google is designed to crawl and index the Web efficiently and produce much more satisfying search results than existing systems."[3]

What made their search engine, Google, more efficient and able to produce better results?

WHY WEREN'T THE EXISTING SEARCH METHODS THAT GREAT?

Before we consider what made Google more efficient, let's turn the question around and ask why the existing search engines weren't that great. Larry and Sergey noted in their paper that directories, such as Yahoo!, that relied on humans to create search results for specific topics are not objective; they cost a lot of money to create and update; and they couldn't possibly cover all topics. The existing automated search engines that just relied on matching keywords entered into the search box with keywords in a document didn't yield high-quality results. Furthermore, spammers could trick automated search results so that instead of getting pure information, search results might be heavily laden with garbage.

Larry and Sergey pointed out in their paper that, in addition to these problems inherent to directories and current search engines, future search engines would have to address the problem of the rapidly growing number of pages to be searched for information and the increasing number of searches taking place daily. These were issues of scale or the size of the tasks.

With Google, Larry and Sergey were able to crawl the Web quickly to not only gather data but to keep it up to date. They were also able to handle search queries quickly. Their primary goal for Google, though, was to improve the quality of search results. This had become less of a priority for some existing companies for whom generating methods to make money off search had become a higher priority. Most providers of search services thought that the existing quality of search was adequate.

Larry and Sergey felt that what was critically needed in search was a way to ensure that users received the most relevant information to meet their search needs. Larry and Sergey set high standards for Google's performance. In their paper, they stated, "we want our notion of 'relevant' to only include the very best documents since there may be tens of thousands of slightly relevant documents." In 2005, during an informal guest appearance in a University of California, Berkeley course called Search Engines: Technology, Society & Business, which was recorded on video, Sergey described their goal at the outset as being able to return search results good enough to satisfy a king or a queen.[4] They initially focused on being able to return the best search results for one person or a small group to perfect the process, but soon they realized they could increase the scale of their computer system to meet the demands of more users.

The primary means by which Larry and Sergey were able to deliver higher quality search results was through the search algorithm they developed called PageRank. Google describes PageRank as "the heart of our software" on its current Web site. This is how PageRank works:

> PageRank relies on the uniquely democratic nature of the web by using its vast link structure as an indicator of an individual page's value. In essence, Google interprets a link from page A to page B as a vote, by page A, for page B. But, Google looks at considerably more than the sheer volume of votes, or links a page receives; for example, it also analyzes the page that casts the vote. Votes cast by pages that are themselves "important" weigh more heavily and help to make other pages "important." Using these and other factors, Google provides its views on pages' relative importance.[5]

Why did Larry and Sergey think that giving searchers the best possible search results was of such critical importance?

Let's step back in time to 1998 to get a feel for what search was like before Google. Scott Rosenberg, managing editor for the online magazine

Salon at that time, provided an analysis of the prevalent search engines of his day and what he wanted from search.

> I am an Internet user. And I resent that today's portals are so obsessed with fine-tuning their demographics and matching every dubious feature their competitors offer that they are doing virtually nothing to improve the service at the heart of all their businesses: helping us all find stuff on the Web.[6]

With Google, Larry and Sergey were determined to address the real need for high-quality search results.

PEOPLE STARTED BUZZING AROUND GOOGLE

In 1997, Larry and Sergey made Google available to the Stanford University community. Google started to gather a following as students, faculty, and administrators used it and liked it. Google became popular at Stanford because people talked about it. The reason they talked about it was because Google gave them good search results—better results than any other search engine. Google continues to rely on the word getting spread from user to user instead of advertising. In the early lean days, not having to spend advertising dollars to develop their brand name and to lure traffic to their site meant a lot to the young company.

They introduced information about their development of Google as presenters at Stanford's Wednesday afternoon Computer Systems Laboratory Colloquium on September 23, 1998. The title of the talk was "Google and the WebBase: What Can You Do with a Web in Your Pocket?"

In the description of their presentation, written before it was given, they promised "to discuss our experiences with the WebBase and Google and we will talk about where this technology will go in the future when all of human knowledge will fit in your shirt pocket."[7]

Their presentation was a success and encouraged more people to spread the word about Google on campus. In their small comfortable university world, they were able to test Google, and they were encouraged by the enthusiastic e-mail they received from people who used Google as their primary search engine.

Shortly after they had incorporated Google and moved off campus using Bechtolsheim's $100,000 in seed money and money from family and friends, Larry and Sergey were handling 100,000 search queries per day. Google's use had grown without any advertising except a newsletter to friends and users. Amazingly enough, over the years, Google continued to gather its ever-growing audience of users without any advertising—it just grew by word of mouth and media attention. Being included in

PC Magazine's list of Top 100 Web Sites and Search Engines for 1998 also boosted Google's visibility and credibility.

BUILDING GOOGLE'S INFRASTRUCTURE

Larry and Sergey continued to improve their search engine to get the most relevant results. They also continued to index Web pages, giving users access to more of the content of the Web over time. By November 1999, Google had crawled 200 million Web pages, 100 million of which were available to users. Google was answering over four million searches per day.

Google's home page was clean and uncluttered, free of ads and banners. Users liked the search box being obvious, right in the middle of the page.

Larry and Sergey increased their infrastructure to 2,000 PCs in their network in 1999. They had 50 people working for them, 30 of whom were engineers, and they had formed a new research group within Google.

Google grew as Larry and Sergey used their experience of successfully cobbling together a computer system in their dorm room and their increased staff and capital to create a bigger system of inexpensive PCs. They were able to keep the costs of their system low by customizing the PCs. Google's Web site explains what this meant for users:

> Google runs on a unique combination of advanced hardware and software. The speed you experience can be attributed in part to the efficiency of our search algorithm and partly to the thousands of low cost PC's we've networked together to create a superfast search engine.[8]

Speed in delivery of search results is critical. If users have to wait too long to get their results, they'll consider leaving a site to conduct their searches elsewhere.

Google has excelled over time in building a network of computers faster and at a lower cost than its competitors. In 2001, it had 8,000 computers at work, up from 2,000 in 1999. The number grew to 100,000 by 2003. The best guess now is 450,000 computers located in at least 25 countries. Major centers in Ireland and Atlanta, Georgia, are connected by a high-capacity fiber optic network.

And, in more recent news, there are reports about new centers in Oklahoma, Iowa, Washington, and South Carolina and plans for an Asian center, among other locations. The cost of these data centers runs about $600 million each. But having more data centers means centers are closer to users and that, too, contributes to fast search results. It also builds redundancy into the system, so that if one center fails or has a power outage, another center can pick up the slack. Google's ongoing investment in data centers and wireless devices positions it to continue to offer the best search results to more people.

Google's computer infrastructure has cost millions of dollars rather than tens of millions of dollars because it used relatively inexpensive machines, designed some of the software in house to make it run efficiently, and used free open-source software.

Open-Source Software

Open-source software is software for which the underlying code, or source code, is available for free to anyone to read it and modify it. Most often, it is created collaboratively by programmers. Changes to an existing open-source code are then shared. Linux is an example of an open-source code that Google uses.

It will be difficult for a new company or an existing competitor to build a comparable system for so little money. The quality of Google's search results, the speed with which it delivers them, as well as its ability to support new services such as video are enough to daunt competitors. Microsoft certainly could bankroll a comparable system and intends to try. Microsoft's computer system currently consists of 200,000 computers, but it hopes to increase that number to 800,000 by 2011.

As of February 2008, Google held 77.27% of the global search engine market, Yahoo! Held 12.23%, and MSN had 3.51%. Clearly, at this point in time, none of the competition is even coming close to Google. Because most people are using Google to search for information, wouldn't advertisers want to place ads on Google?

GOOGLE STARTS TO DEVELOP A BUSINESS STRATEGY

By November 1999, in a response in a *Washington Post* interview about the source of Google's income, Sergey said that its income at that point was "from cobranding with partners like Netscape and RedHat" and that they had "about 10" distribution and revenue partners, including the *Washington Post*. He also reported that an advertising pilot program was underway.[9]

Larry and Sergey felt strongly about maintaining the integrity of search for their users. While other companies sold banner ads, text, and graphic ads that appeared on their pages of search results, Larry and Sergey resisted mixing search and advertising. They were especially vehement in their resistance to search results having ads mixed in with them so that sometimes the searcher wasn't aware that a search result that appeared in the top search results was paid for rather than showing up because it was the most relevant result for their query.

Although Google was generating some revenue, it needed more to stay alive and to grow. In June 1999, Google received $25 million in venture funding from Sequoia Capital and Kleiner Perkins Caufield & Byers.

Sequoia Capital and Kleiner Perkins Caufield & Byers

Sequoia Capital and Kleiner Perkins Caufield & Byers are two of the leading U.S. venture capital firms specializing in providing venture capital to technology companies in their early stages of development. They both have consistently picked some big winners to back, and Google was one of those winners.

In addition to Google, Sequoia Capital worked with Apple, Oracle, Cisco, Yahoo!, and YouTube, among others. It invests in services, software, systems, and components and selects fast growing companies for investment. It has been the first venture capital investor in companies that comprise 10% of the NASDAQ's value.

Michael Mortiz of Sequoia Capital, who supported Larry and Sergey and provided them management expertise in their early days, has been named number one on *Forbes'* Midas List more than once. (The Midas List ranks the top tech dealmakers in the world.) Moritz studied history at Oxford University, and then became a journalist. He also worked several different positions with Time Warner and was a founder of Technologic Partners. In the 1980s, he became a venture capitalist and concentrated on software and services investments.

John Doerr of Kleiner Perkins Caufield & Byers, who also supported Google with venture capital, was named number one on the Midas List for 2007. Doerr earned a masters of business administration degree from Harvard Business School after graduating with a masters of science degree in electrical engineering and computer science and a bachelor of science degree in electrical engineering from Rice University. He has served on Google's board of directors since 1999.

Kleiner Perkins Caufield & Byers has invested in information technology companies since its founding in 1972. Sun, Symantec, Netscape, and Amazon represent some of its investments. Currently, it concentrates on innovations in "greentech," life sciences, and ideas and products that extend the new iPhone and iPod touch platform.

The infusion of capital made it possible for Google to hire Omid Kordestani away from Netscape as its vice president of business development and sales. Urs Hölzle left the University of California, Santa Barbara to join Google as vice president of engineering. Both continue to make significant contributions to Google's success.

Google was also able to move into larger space, the Googleplex, in Mountain View, California, where its staff could grow to meet the demands of new clients. The demand for its service jumped past three million searches a day when it signed on to provide Web search service to AOL/Netscape. International visibility and traffic increased when Virgin Net, the leading online UK entertainment guide, and Virgilio, an Italian portal for the Web, became clients for Google's Web search service.

Google showed up on some "best of" lists, including *Time* magazine's Top Ten Best Cybertech list. *PC Magazine* gave it its Technical Excellence Award for Innovation in Web Application Development. This was all great free publicity for the company as well as recognition of their accomplishments.

Google began to create its global market by introducing 10 language versions so users could search in their native languages. Google is now available in 35 languages. This was a service that had been largely overlooked by competitors before Google provided it to a growing world audience.

Google's search services were extended in 1999 with the ability to search using wireless devices. This was the year that Google officially became the world's largest search engine with its billion-page index.

GOOGLE DEVELOPS REVENUE STREAMS

Larry and Sergey acknowledged that Google had to make money to stay alive, but they were committed to making money "without doing evil," as they put it. Google initiated two strategies to bring in revenue in 1999 to 2000 that enabled them to show a profit for the first time. Over time, these strategies generated impressive profits. The first strategy was that clients paid to use Google's search technology on their own sites. A partnership with Yahoo! was a huge coup for Google, and it was followed by a partnership deal with China's leading portal as well as a prominent portal in Japan. With new partnerships in 2001, Google extended search to Sprint PCS, Cingular, and AT&T Wireless customers.

Google's Entry into the Chinese Market

Google's deal with NetEase was the first step in building its brand name in China. China represents a huge market for any U.S. company, and Google has continued to try to capture the market there. We'll learn more about Google in China in a later chapter. But at this point in time, it offered Chinese language search through NetEase. NetEase attracted Chinese users by offering e-mail, news, chat, and auctions. NetEase was able to offer its 5.9 million users more than 24 million Chinese language Web pages through its agreement with Google. In July 2007, NetEase started to use its own search engine and ended its agreement with Google.

In 2002, building on its search competency, Google created Google Search Appliances for organizations. This enabled organizations to search their own documents and other information sources while keeping their intranets secure. The appliances integrate software and hardware with Web-based interfaces and the Google user interface. The World Bank, the U.S. Army, the U.S. Department of the Treasury, NASA, Apple Computer, PBS, Procter & Gamble, Timex Corporation, Eli Lilly & Company, National Geographic, Cisco Systems, many colleges and universities, and local governments are just a sample of the organizations that use Google Appliances.

The second revenue stream was from advertisers paying to display ads next to search results on Google and content partner sites that were relevant to their products. Google's proprietary technology facilitated the precise matching of ads to content. Google was careful to separate search results from ads to avoid distracting users and to keep search results pure. Ads appeared on the right-hand side of the screen away from search results on the left. Because they were able to match the kind of ad that appeared so well with content, many users actually found these ads helpful.

About $20 billion is spent on Internet advertising in the United States, drawing money away from traditional advertisers such as TV and print media. A significant reason for this switch is that Google has been able to deliver good returns to those who place their ads there. Google has successfully targeted its advertisers' markets by matching ads to keyword searches.

Google extended this advertising model to other media, such as cell phones and, more recently, to video on its subsidiary, YouTube. It also offers advertising through Google Print Ads Program, Google Audio Ads, and Google TV Ads. Although Google Print Ads is not auction based like its Internet advertising program, advertisers can propose what they want to pay to publishers participating in the program with Google. Publishers can accept or reject the offer. The process takes place online, and Google bills advertisers once a month. It is a variation of Google's Internet advertising model of connecting advertisers with media in which to place their ads.

For radio ads, Google has partnered with over 1,600 AM/FM U.S. stations. Companies who want to advertise bid on 30-second slots online through an AdWords account and decide where they want their ads to air. Participants who don't want to bid but who want to reserve time at a set price, can also do that through Google.

Google began testing Google TV Ads with invited participants in June 2007. In May 2008, it opened the program to all advertisers. To attract advertisers, for a limited period of time, Google will pay advertisers who don't have TV ads up to $2,000 on the cost of creating a TV ad through its Ad Creation Marketplace. If advertisers are uncertain of how to reach their audiences, they can request a free customized campaign proposal based on audience demographics. Advertisers use Google's AdWords to bid on the maximum cost per thousand impressions they are willing to pay. Advertisers only pay when their ads air.

Through variations of its AdWords program, Google is attempting to serve advertisers across all media—the Internet, print, radio, and television. Television advertising alone is a multibillion-dollar market, and Google's brand name and success with Internet advertising will help it attract advertisers. Furthermore, its advertisers who have already been using AdWords for advertising on the Internet can use their same accounts to buy advertising across all media. The potential for additional revenue for Google from these additional media is immense. It is creating one-stop shopping for advertising.

Google currently makes considerably more money from advertising connected to search results than it does from software licensing and other products. In 2007, it made $16.4 billion from advertising and just $181 million from software licensing and selling its other products.

GOOGLE'S NEW PRODUCT DEVELOPMENT MODEL

Google's approach to new product development is to rapidly offer a prototype. It offers it to the wide Google search audience public for free to work out the kinks in it and to get user feedback. Then, if it's appropriate, Google engineers refine it and customize it before offering an enterprise edition for businesses, governments, and other large organizations. For example, over the past two years, it has offered free programs for word processing and spreadsheets. The programs that can be downloaded from the Google Web site are available to anyone in the world with an Internet connection and a computer with the capacity to run them. This approach is distinct from Microsoft, the market leader in this area, which charges for these products, which require installation on individual computers. Microsoft upgrades must be purchased and installed again on individual computers.

Google's enterprise versions of these products, which it does sell, have the potential to challenge Microsoft's market dominance. Currently, more than 500,000 schools, government agencies, and companies use some of its applications.

Another example of products offered both free and to enterprises is Google Maps, which offers users a way to get directions and find businesses and other places of interest. It is free to users, and businesses can add their locations to maps for a fee.

In 2004, Google acquired Keyhole Corporation, a digital and satellite image mapping company that allowed users to search three-dimensional images across the earth. On top of this acquisition, Google Earth was created, which can simulate flight. Users can zoom in on specific places for a closer look.

Google has developed geospatial solutions for businesses based on these products. Google Maps API is free. But some businesses needed more, and Google developed an enterprise version. Google Maps API Premier includes all the interactive features of Google Maps, but it is designed to return rapid and relevant results for high-traffic Web sites and to give businesses control over advertising within the maps customers select. It is used, for example, by retail stores that have many locations to provide maps and directions to customers to find locations near them. Real estate companies also use it to show locations of properties for sale. Large travel companies can use it to provide information to clients.

GOOGLE BUILDS A GLOBAL LEARNING COMMUNITY

One of Google's core principles is an unwavering commitment to the needs of the end user. Within the huge Google community of users are smaller communities of users who use Google's services and products for specific purposes. Google listens to its huge community and to the voices of the smaller communities within it. It listens to what users want and need by creating the means for users to provide feedback on its Web site. Google learns from its users and tries to implement their suggestions. In this way, Google has created an interactive learning community around its products and services built on two-way communication on its site. This model includes search and free tools for the average Google user as well as its products and services for small and large businesses. Google is sensitive to the fact that small businesses have different needs and budgets from large businesses and tries to accommodate them with some free products and reasonably priced products.

Google has, from its beginning, had a special relationship with the technology community of engineers, programmers, and Web masters. This community tries out early versions of Google products at Google's request and provides valuable suggestions for improvement and innovation. Google has acknowledged the tech community's contribution by sponsoring programming contests with prizes for engineers and by offering Web masters free tools to improve and analyze their sites. Larry and Sergey are strong advocates of open-source code, and they make some of their code available on their site and invite programmers to use it and to share their use of it with Google's engineers.

This strong connection to its users is not only necessary to feed innovation and to anticipate the needs of users, it creates a strategic advantage. Google has created a direct pipeline to its users, and, by finding out what they like and don't like and making adjustments, it retains and builds its audience for advertising.

GOOGLE'S IPO BRINGS VINDICATION

Larry and Sergey, with the help of CEO Eric Schmidt, guided Google successfully as a private company, which generated a profit in 2001. Their strategies of concentrating on providing end users with the most relevant results to their searches tied to relevant unobtrusive ads had paid off for them. This became evident when financial information about the company was revealed when they provided details for their initial public offering (IPO) and later went public.

Initial Public Offering

An initial public offering (IPO) is the first sale of stock by a private company to the public. IPOs are often issued by new, young companies seeking capital to grow. Sometimes older companies that have been privately held for long periods of time decide to issue an IPO as well to expand, diversify, or for other reasons. The money from an IPO goes directly to the company. Shares traded on the stock market subsequently are traded between investors unless a company issues stock again at some point. Companies will issue more shares to raise money without borrowing it. This is one reason companies will decide to transition from being privately held to being a publicly traded company—access to capital without having to borrow it. It also means they don't have to find private investors if they need capital.

When Google filed its IPO in April 2004, it recorded revenues of $961.9 million with a net profit of $106.5 million for the previous year. For the first quarter of 2004, sales increased by 118% from the previous year. Net income was $64 million, an increase of 148% from the first quarter of 2003. This was a very strong showing for a young company; its sales grew in the first quarter at a higher rate than both Yahoo! and eBay.[10]

Its first day of public trading yielded $1.67 billion, of which $1.2 billion went back into the company and $473 million went to Google executives and investors who sold their shares.[11] The price set for its stock was $85 per share. By the end of the day, it was trading for $100.

The company was valued, after its first day of trading, at more than $27 billion, exceeding the market value of companies such as Amazon, General Motors, and Lockheed Martin. Not only were Larry and Sergey now billionaires, approximately 1,000 Googlers out of the 2,300 employees were now millionaires.[12]

Google's unique corporate structure and corporate culture are a huge part of what has made it a successful company. We'll take a look at both in the next chapter.

NOTES

1. "Our Philosophy," Google Corporate Information, http://www.google.com/corporate/tenthings.html (accessed March 5, 2008).

2. Ibid.

3. Sergey Brin and Lawrence Page, "The Anatomy of a Large-Scale Hypertextual Web Search Engine," Stanford University InfoLab, http://infolab.stanford.edu/~ backrub/google.html (accessed February 10, 2008).

4. "Sergey Brin Speaks with UC Berkeley Class," Google Video, http://video.google.com/videoplay?docid=7582902000166025817 (accessed March 1, 2008).

5. "Our Search: Google Technology," http://www.google.com/technology (accessed March 25, 2008).

6. Scott Rosenberg, "Yes, There *Is* a Better Search Engine," *Salon 21st,* http://archive.salon.com/21st/rose/1998/12/21straight.html (accessed May 13, 2008).

7. http://www.stanford.edu/class/ee380 (accessed February 21, 2008).

8. "Our Search: Google Technology," http://www.google.com/technology (accessed February 7, 2008).

9. Leslie Walker, *Washington Post*.com-LIVE, November 4, 1999, http://www.washingtonpost.com/wp-srv/liveonline/business/walker/walker110499.htm (accessed March 10, 2008).

10. Paul R. La Monica, "Google Sets $2.7 Billion IPO: Popular Search Engine Company Files for Its Eagerly Anticipated Initial Public Offering," CNN Money.com, April 30, 2004, http://money.cnn.com/2004/04/29/technology/google (accessed March 5, 2008).

11. "Google IPO Priced at $85 a Share: Troubled Stock Debut To Go Ahead Thursday," CNN.com, August 19, 2004, http://edition.cnn.com/2004/BUSINESS/08/19/google.ipo (accessed March 7, 2008).

12. Gary Rivlin, "After Months of Hoopla, Google Debut Fits the Norm," *New York Times,* August 20, 2004, http://www.nytimes.com/2004/08/20/technology/20google.html?ex=1250740800&en=856f04ed73aef6fd&ei=5090&partner=rssuserl and (accessed March 9, 2008).

Chapter Five

The Wonderful World of Work and Play at Google

We don't just want you to have a great job. We want you to have a great life. We provide you with everything you need to be productive and happy on and off the clock.[1]

Larry Page, Google cofounder

With that kind of dedication to its employees, is it any wonder that Google was voted the number one company to work for in the United States in 2006 and 2007 by *Fortune* magazine? Yahoo! was 44th on the list for 2007, and Microsoft was 50th. Genetech, a company that Larry and Sergey admire, held the number one ranking the year before Google. Genetech's CEO and Google board member Art Levinson commented to *Fortune* that "What draws people to both companies is the environment, one where they have an ability to pursue things largely on their own terms."[2]

How the Best Companies Are Picked by *Fortune*

Fortune partners with the Great Place to Work Institute to administer an extensive employee survey that consists of 57 questions. In 2007, 446 companies participated, and over 100,000 employees were surveyed. *Fortune* and the Great Place to Work Institute send the survey to at least 400 randomly selected employees of a given company. The results of the survey make up two-thirds of the company's score. The Great Place to Work Institute conducts a "culture audit" to produce the remaining third of the score. This audit considers diversity programs, the pay and benefits program, as well as the answers to more general questions about management's philosophy and the nature of communication within the company.[3]

What is it about Google that makes it such a great place to work? How does the structure of the company and the work environment contribute to its success? To answer these questions, let's first take a look at Google's corporate culture.

BUILDING A CORPORATE CULTURE TO CREATE STRATEGIC ADVANTAGE

Right before Google made the transition from a private company to a public company, Larry and Sergey composed a letter to potential investors to make it clear that the workplace atmosphere and management of Google were different and that they intended for it to stay that way. They stated this clearly in this excerpt from the letter: "Google is not a conventional company. We do not intend to become one. Throughout Google's evolution as a privately held company, we have managed Google differently. We have also emphasized an atmosphere of creativity and challenge, which has helped us provide unbiased, accurate and free access to information for those who rely on us around the world."[4]

The culture of a corporation is created by its mission, its philosophy, the spirits of the founders, and the combined interactive energy of the people who are the corporation. A corporation's culture is reflected in the quality of its products and services, its physical environment, and the dedication and enthusiasm of its employees to meeting the company's mission. The strategic advantage that a company creates based on its culture is the final word in the marketplace on the success of that culture.

Google's Corporate Information Web page states its mission so simply; yet this mission is a monumental task, an ongoing quest for Larry and Sergey and their employees, the Googlers:

> Google's mission is to organize the world's information and make it universally accessible and useful.[5]

At Google, this mission is the Tao, the force, the true reality behind everything the company does. It lives in the collective consciousness of Googlers as they go about their work moving the company and the world closer to this goal that can be approached but never quite reached. Unlike other search engines that came before it, Google's commitment to making the best search engine and producing the best results for search in order to meet its mission has never wavered.

THE GOOGLE PHILOSOPHY

Google offers insights about its philosophy on the corporate page of its Web site (www.google.com/corporate/tenthings.html) under the heading "Ten Things Google Has Found To Be True."

1. Focus on the User and All Else Will Follow

From their early days at Stanford, Larry and Sergey wanted to create the best search experience for their users. This continued to be their first priority after they formed a company. They consider four components essential to the best search experience: a user interface that is easy to use, high-speed return of search results, pure ranking of search results rather than selling ranking, and only ads that are unobtrusive and relevant to the search being undertaken. These four components, they seem to rightly believe, build trust in Google search results and a devoted global community of users who use Google for search rather than any other search engine.

2. It's Best To Do One Thing Really, Really Well

Search remains the core competency of Google and it continues to devote time, personnel, and dollars to improve it. Products such as Google Maps and Gmail were built on that competency, and the company continues to seek ways to develop new products based on its knowledge derived from the problem-solving techniques developed from its commitment to continuous improvement of search.

3. Fast Is Better than Slow

Google recognizes that its users want instant gratification. So it continues to work on making search results return to the user faster both through its networked PCs and improved algorithms.

4. Democracy on the Web Works

Larry and Sergey's original research led them to understand the link structure of the Web as a democratic system. By analyzing the quality of the links to a particular site with their PageRank algorithm and other methods, they've been able to determine "which sites have been 'voted' the best sources of information" by other sites.

5. You Don't Need To Be at Your Desk To Need an Answer

Google recognizes that people need information wherever they are. It is committed to researching and providing the best options for search for wireless devices.

6. You Can Make Money without Doing Evil

Google believes that money can be made honestly by only displaying ads on a search results page if they are relevant to the topic for which a search is being conducted. Google also believes in simple text ads to the right of the screen that don't obscure the pure search results. An ad is distinctly labeled as a sponsored link on Google search results pages. And no one can buy a rank in the pure search results.

7. There's Always More Information Out There

Google indexes more pages written in HTML than any other search provider. Not satisfied with that, it initiated ways to search for images and other file formats like PDF, PowerPoint, and Microsoft Word. Google made it possible for mobile devices to translate HTML.

8. The Need for Information Crosses All Borders

Google serves the world by offering a translation feature as well as by giving users the option to restrict search results to pages written in 35 native languages of their choice. Customization of its user interface is possible in more than 100 languages.

9. You Can Be Serious without a Suit

Larry and Sergey "built a company around the idea that work should be challenging and the challenge should be fun." The corporate culture they've created is built on the wish to keep Googlers happy and creative in a team environment while still recognizing individual contributions as well. "This highly communicative environment fosters a productivity and camaraderie fueled by the realization that millions of people rely on Google results. Give the proper tools to a group of people who like to make a difference, and they will."

10. Great Just Isn't Good Enough

Google tries to stay ahead of the curve by anticipating what its users will need. In this sense, it is never satisfied but always seeking to raise the bar.[6]

GOOGLE'S MOTTO

"Don't be evil" is the Google motto, and it shapes how Google meets it mission, how decisions are made, and the conduct of Googlers. The following excerpt from a September 2004 *Playboy* interview with Sergey and Larry shortly before Google made the transition from a private company to a public company clarifies what this motto means.

> *Brin:* As for "Don't be evil," we have tried to define precisely what it means to be a force for good—always do the right, ethical thing. Ultimately, "Don't be evil" seems the easiest way to summarize it.
>
> *Page:* Apparently people like it better than "Be good."
>
> *Brin:* It's not enough not to be evil. We also actively try to be good.

Later in the same interview, Sergey noted that this policy frequently sparks discussions within the company about the precise nature of evil and how to avoid it as they make business choices. He connects the motto with the company's mission to make all the information in the world available to everyone. Google management and Googlers extensively research everything related to their own decisions about what products and services to develop not only to develop excellent products and services, but to avoid doing evil as well. As Sergey commented later in the *Playboy* interview, "One thing we know is that people can make better decisions with better information."[7]

More recently, in the January 12, 2008, edition of the *Business Times,* Singapore, Vikram Khanna asked Eric Schmidt, Google's CEO, for his interpretation of the motto in an interview. It's clear from Schmidt's comments that he understands how important this motto is to Larry and Sergey and to Google's corporate culture. It is also important to the public image they want to create for Google.

Schmidt admits that, when he first came to Google, he thought the motto was a joke. But then in a meeting when a debate over whether a new ad product would be good or evil went on for an hour, he realized that it was not a joke. He goes on to comment on the value of the motto and elaborates on what it means.

> ...the way "don't be evil" plays out is that it forces the question, it forces the debate....in general we would say, more information is good and things which are positive for end users are good. So we're always concerned about things that restrict information and which prevent people from having choices.[8]

"Don't Be Evil"—Part of the Google Code of Conduct

"'Don't be evil.' Googlers generally apply those words to how we serve our users. But 'Don't be evil' is much more than that. Yes, it's about providing our users unbiased access to information, focusing on their needs and giving them the best products and services that we can. But it's also about doing the right thing more generally—following the law, acting honorably and treating each other with respect.

The Google Code of Conduct is one of the ways we put 'Don't be evil' into practice. It's built around the recognition that everything we do in connection with our work at Google will be, and should be, measured against the highest possible standards of ethical business conduct. We set the bar that high for practical as well as aspirational reasons: We hire great people who work hard to build great products, and it's essential that we build an environment of trust—among ourselves and with our users. That trust and mutual respect underlie our success, and we need to earn it every day."[9]

Google nurtures an enlightened corporate culture that is based on a commitment to excellence in search and an ethical code based not only on "Don't be evil" but also on doing good in the world. We'll learn more about how Google does good in the world in the chapter about philanthropy.

This corporate culture creates considerable competitive advantage for the company by helping it to recruit and keep the best employees who will dedicate themselves to the company's mission. It is the basis for the work environment that is fueled by idealism and cooperation to create new products and services, to improve existing ones, and to solve problems.

NURTURING THE CORPORATE CULTURE

Stacy Savides Sullivan is director of human resources at Google and chief culture officer. Her comments in a 2007 interview with Elinor Mills of CNET News.com indicate just how important the Google culture is to meeting the mission of the company and how she helps to both preserve and develop it. Google is trying to meet the challenge of transplanting its culture to its offices in other cities in the United States and in other parts of the world. She comments that she "works with employees around the world to figure out ways to maintain and enhance and develop our culture and how to keep the core values we had in the very beginning—a flat organization, a lack of hierarchy, a collaborative environment....We want all of our employees to play a part in being involved in keeping our culture the way it is today but also growing and developing it."[10]

What Does the Google Culture Look Like in India?

If you're roaming a work environment that has lava lamps, beanbag chairs, massage chairs, as well as play areas with foosball and billiards interspersed with powerful computer work stations, you know enough by now to guess that you're in the Googleplex, right? But what if you also see cricket jerseys on walls and a chair with a tent over with a sign declaring that fortunes are told there? Maybe you're not in Mountain View, California, after all!

As it has opened offices around the world, Google has been challenged to transplant its California-born culture to other cultures. In its research center in Bangalore, India, there is strong evidence that its unique culture has been transferred, but there is also evidence that it has been influenced by the culture of India as well. Aside from the décor already described, there's also the free food that Google offers all Googlers, but along with the candy and Pringles there is chaat and local fried snacks. Naturally, the cafeteria offers Indian curries.

The transfer of Google culture to India was easier than it might have been, because some of the Indian Googlers returned to India to be a part of the new research center's startup after working in the Mountain View Googleplex. Add to this the fact that Google is the most popular search engine in India, making it easier for the company to recruit new talent than its competitors Yahoo! and Microsoft. Google offers salaries that are around three times higher than its competitors as well. And, because Google is so popular and well respected by Indians, marriage opportunities abound for unmarried Indian Googlers. Google receives thousands of job applications per month for positions in the research center.

Google replicated its casual college campus atmosphere in India because it believes that when Googlers are well fed, comfortable, relaxed, and happy innovation and creativity are nurtured. A. C. Narendran, who worked for Google in California before returning to India, explains with good humor the effect that the atmosphere has on Googlers in India. "These games and lounge chairs clearly send the message that folks are not expected to do any work here, and software engineers being contrarian in their thinking go and do the opposite—which is to work all the time."[11]

When asked how she would characterize the Google culture, Sullivan responded that it is "team-oriented, very collaborative" and that people are "encouraged to think nontraditionally...working with integrity and for the good of the company and for the good of the world, which is tied to our overall mission of making information accessible to the world."[12] The characteristics of the Google culture, as Sullivan describes it, are what have helped to make Google one of the most productive and innovative technology think tanks in the world. Devoting time, money, resources, and thought to nurturing this culture have been good investments for Google.

WHAT'S IT LIKE TO WORK AT GOOGLE?

Imagine that you're on your way to work at Google. From your home in San Francisco, you hop on a Google-chartered bus fueled by biodiesel and equipped with wireless access to the Internet. You get a jump on your work day by checking your e-mail on the way to the Googleplex in Mountain View, California. You had to skip breakfast because you were late getting up, but you're not worried because you can get a free breakfast at work—and free lunch and dinner. Once you arrive at the Googleplex, which resembles a college campus, you head for breakfast at Charlie's Café.

If you had worked at the Googleplex before May 2005, you would have been able to enjoy the exquisite cuisine of legendary head chef Charlie Ayers, former occasional chef for members of the Grateful Dead band. Ayers was loved and respected at Google.

Chef Charlie, as Charlie Ayers came to be known at Google, made a huge, healthy, and yummy contribution to the Google culture as well as to its worldwide image during his almost six-year tenure at the company. In the early days of Google, Larry and Sergey got a lot of recruiting mileage out of Charlie's previous work experience cooking for members of the Grateful Dead. But it wasn't long before Charlie's nurturing gourmet food and warm personality created even more good PR for Google.

Sergey had a vision of providing employees with free healthy meals even before Google was a year old. Good food powered good thinking and good work. Providing free food on site cut down time away from the building getting food. And employees could share ideas and build a sense of community while happily eating healthy gourmet meals.

Sergey invited Charlie to the downtown Palo Alto office that provided tight quarters for a dozen employees to share his vision and offer him a job as company chef. At that point, Charlie was skeptical—and with good cause, because the offices didn't even have a kitchen, and there weren't enough employees to justify hiring a chef.

But less than a year later, after Google had moved to Mountain View and had grown to more than 40 employees, Charlie answered an ad for a chef posted on the Google Web site. Google had interviewed quite a few chefs, but no one suited the company and its needs. Charlie was hired in November 1999. He began to work on a shared vision with Larry and Sergey to provide Googlers with free, healthy food. Over the next four years, he built the reputation of Google for having the best free meals in the Silicon Valley.

Charlie's meals nurtured the Googlers and became the centerpiece of the unique perks Google offered its family to attract new hires. Sample menus were posted on its Web site as part of its recruiting effort. The free lunch was listed as one of the "Top 10 Reasons to Work at Google" that is also posted on the Web site.

Over time, Charlie created meals that were Earth-friendly, using more organic ingredients and biodegradable flatware. To meet the needs of the diversity of the Google community, his menus included Asian, Indian, Middle Eastern, and Italian dishes, among others. But one of his most popular dishes, which he'd learned about from a former cook for Elvis Presley in another job, was fried chicken based on a recipe that was one of Elvis's favorites and that Charlie describes in his Google blog. The recipe called for marinating the chicken in buttermilk for several days. It also called for just about every spice under the sun.

Not only did he oversee the preparation of meals, Chef Charlie planned the food for the TGIF parties and, at times, hired the live entertainment for these occasions and created themes for the parties.

When Charlie started with Google, he did everything himself in a small electric kitchen. By the time he left the company in May 2005, he oversaw a kitchen staff of 135, serving 4,000 meals a day in a state-of-the art kitchen.

He also cooked for a variety of famous visitors to the Googleplex such as Bill Clinton, Jimmy Carter, Al Gore, Madeleine Albright, Colin Powell, Mikhail Gorbachev, the sultan of Brunei, Queen Noor of Jordan, Robin Williams, Bono, The Edge, Coldplay, and Gwyneth Paltrow. The *New York Times, London Times,* France's *Le Capital,* the *Washington Post, Food Management, Restaurants Institutions,* the Food Network, and many others featured him, his food, and his Google cafés. David Vise devoted a chapter in his book, *The Google Story,* to Charlie and what he accomplished at Google.

Currently, Chef Charlie notes on his Web site that he is available for "innovative corporate well-being" consulting, which consists of "restructuring corporate food service programs and designing Micro Kitchen/Food Service programs tailored to fit the individual company's size and desired corporate culture."[13]

He is also "developing a new restaurant concept that will demonstrate that 'being green' is good for the consumer, team members, environment, and local community." He plans to open his own restaurant, called the Calafia Café & Market a Go Go, in Palo Alto "to provide the greater public with healthful, artisan-style, sustainable cuisine in a fast and affordable format" in 2008. Chef Charlie wrote a cookbook that came out in spring 2008 called *Food 2.0: Secrets from the Chef Who Fed Google.* He devotes time to nonprofit charitable organizations such ChefsForHumanity.org and ROCKtheEARTH.org, sitting on their advisory boards.

Google currently has 11 campus cafes, each with its own executive chef. Café150 opened recently that supports organic farming by using products raised within 150 miles of the Googleplex.

The Political and Economic Implications of Google's Commitment to Local Food

Google is committed to providing healthy and delicious meals to Googlers. When Larry and Sergey looked for a replacement for Charlie Ayers, they looked for someone who would carry on his legacy of Earth-friendly food service. They hired John Dickman, a former manager at catering giant Bon Appetit Management Co. to become Google's global food service manager in 2004. While he continues to buy organic when he can, Dickman has shifted the focus to buying local as being more important. He commented in a *Time* magazine article relative to buying organic nectarines from Chile, "You're using X amount of jet fuel to get it here, and that doesn't make sense. So forget the nectarines. Buy something local."[14]

Google's commitment to buying local and the amount of money it spends on food is having a positive effect on small produce farms and may impact how much agricultural land in the area is spared development. It is also modeling for other large institutions a new concept and a new set of standards for corporate responsibility in terms of the quality of food it feeds its employees and its awareness of the local economy. Aside from Google, Bon Appetit and two major universities in the area are now buying local food. Brian Gardiner, who founded America Fresh, which distributes produce from small local growers, says that "Google makes a significant difference." According to Gardiner and other local producers, 25% of their income comes from Google and Bon Appetit.[15]

Google has also planted citrus trees at the Googleplex to provide fresh fruit. Diane McClamroch, a member of the food services team at Google, reported in her May 9, 2008, blog that Google celebrated the one-year anniversary of its organic garden. She notes that it is not only a "stunning centerpiece for the central campus," but that the vegetables and herbs grown there are used daily in the Google cafes. She goes on to report that the garden was part of a grass-roots project called Growing Connection started by the United Nation's Food and Agriculture Organization.[16]

The Growing Connection project is based on growing vegetables in an EarthBox, which is a patented growing system that helps growers cultivate produce with limited space and water. Schools and communities around the world grow vegetables using this system. Participating students learn about horticulture and share their experiences with other students around the world using modern IT installations. The technology also enables them to continue to learn about growing food.

Google's organic garden at the Googleplex consists of 100 EarthBoxes planted with vegetables and herbs from around the world.[17]

Meanwhile...back to imagining your day if you worked at Google. After breakfast you pause in the hallway cluttered with bicycles and exercise balls to greet a friend and his dog who has accompanied him to work and to listen to a fragment of a concerto played by a Googler on a baby grand piano in another room. You're passed by another friend who has just come in from jogging on the trails in the complex.

Today, instead of working with your two team members on a collaborative project, you start working on a product idea that might go nowhere. But, as Larry noted in his letter to potential shareholders before Google went public, Googlers are not only free, but encouraged "to spend 20% of their time working on what they think will most benefit Google." He goes on to explain why. "This empowers them to be more creative and innovative. Many of our significant advances have happened in this manner. For example, AdSense for content and Google News were both prototyped in '20% time.' Most risky projects fizzle, often teaching us something. Others succeed and become attractive businesses."[18]

Googlers are encouraged to be fearless in their thinking and experimentation. Richard Holden, product management director for Google's

AdWords service, elaborated on that idea in a *Washington Post* article: "If you're not failing enough, you're not trying hard enough. The stigma [for failure] is less because we staff projects leanly and encourage them to just move, move, move. If it doesn't work, move on."[19]

This forward momentum is essential to a company trying to not only survive in a highly competitive environment, but for one that is trying to maintain its position as the leader in its industry. It requires employees who are agile. Google employees are not hired for one specific project. They get assigned where they are needed. They can also ask to be taken off a project, no questions asked.

At lunch time, you get a massage on site because you're still a little sore from the roller blade hockey game in the parking lot that's roped off twice a week for that purpose. During the game, you cheerfully allowed yourself to be mowed down by a cute Noogler, the Google term for a new employee.

If by now you think this work day is only a fantasy, you're wrong. It's real and what you've experienced in your short fantasy tour is only part of the possible unusual benefits of working at Google. Do you want to know about the snack rooms, the game rooms, the gym, the high-tech toilets, the lap pools? The dress code that simply requires that you wear something? It would seem that nothing is too far-fetched in this environment if it helps to keep Googlers happy. Google openly acknowledges that its employees are the company's most valuable asset. It needs to attract the best in the world and keep them happy so they'll stay. One of the ways it does both is with a generous benefits package.

BENEFITS PACKAGE

Google offers an impressive tangible benefits package that includes medical, dental, and vision insurance and life, accidental death, and long- and short-term disability insurance. A flex spending account plan for health needs, dependent care, and transportation are part of the package. An employee assistance program for employees and dependents includes legal consultations, financial planning, short-term counseling, and child and pet care referrals. The 401(k) plans and college savings plans, generous holiday and sick time, maternity and parental leave, financial assistance for adoption and for buying energy-efficient cars, and a gift-matching program for contributions to charitable organizations are also part of the joys of working at Google. Child care is offered at its child care center, and tuition reimbursement is offered for up to $8,000 a year. Free meals, sports facilities, on-site doctors, off-site trips, and parties are more benefits to convince prospective employees that Google really does care. Eric Schmidt, CEO at Google, sums up the benefits:

> The goal is to strip away everything that gets in our employees way. We provide a standard package of fringe benefits, but on

top of that are first-class dining facilities, gyms, laundry rooms, massage rooms, haircuts, carwashes, dry cleaning, commuting buses—just about anything a hardworking employee engineer might want.[20]

Sergey and Larry, by creating a happy, healthy, collaborative community, are putting in place the cornerstone for a company that can grow and be sustained over time. They have clearly made a choice. Arie de Gues writes in a *Harvard Business Review* article, "The Living Company":

> Managers must decide how to position the human element in their companies. They can choose to provide wealth for an inner circle of managers and investors, or they can develop an organization that is a community. Managers who want to build an organization that can survive many generations pay attention to the development of employees above all other considerations.[21]

WHAT IS MANAGEMENT LIKE AT GOOGLE?

In the now-famous *Playboy* interview given right before the company went public, Larry and Sergey were asked if they adhered to any particular management theories or if they made them up. Larry responded, "We try to use elements from different companies, but a lot is seat-of-your-pants stuff."[22]

Flat Organization

Google is a flat organization—meaning there are few layers of management. Flat organizations work well in environments that need to rapidly produce prototypes, test them, and then decide whether to develop or discard them. The pace of development in a company like Google is probably not for the fainthearted. Hundreds of projects are developed simultaneously by small collaborative teams. A new application is likely to be generated in six weeks or less and then made available to Google users for a response. With over 80 million visitors per month, Google has more than a sufficient audience on which to test a new product.

Google's engineers and product developers are, in a significant way, managed by their peers. This self-management is facilitated by information dissemination and in-house debate driven by data rather than opinion.

Sharing Information Drives Productive Interaction

Sharing information is built into Google's internal communication system. At the beginning of each week, Googlers summarize what they did the week before, and this information is shared on an internal Web site. A mailing list for engineers is the medium through which new product ideas are put out for feedback and invitations to brainstorm are issued.

Group Culture and Decision Making

When CEO Eric Schmidt was asked in an interview whether individuals or groups make decisions at Google, he responded:

> It's a group culture. There are almost no individual decisions.... The really major, major decisions about the company are made by the founders and me—three is better than two. But almost all big decisions are made in groups of 15 or 20, after a long discussion....
>
> The other philosophy we try to adopt is that you don't go for consensus, you go for the best idea, which is different.[23]

This collaborative model based on peer review of projects and advocacy or rejection of projects based on data in group debates empowers Googlers and reduces the number of managers needed.

The teams run their ideas by project managers who serve as mentors. Marissa Mayer, who is currently vice president of search products and user experience, joined Google in 1999 as the first woman engineer. She manages innovation in the search field. Project teams visit her during set office hours reminiscent of her time at Stanford teaching computer science. She is prepared to help solve problems, brainstorm, help with coding— whatever is needed to move a project along. She screens new ideas and decides whether and when they should be presented to Larry and Sergey.

Marissa Mayer, Vice President, Search Products and User Experience

Marissa Mayer first heard about Google when she was 23 and enrolled in the graduate program at Stanford. She came to Stanford from a small town in Wisconsin. Her mom was an art teacher, and her dad was an engineer. In high school, Marissa excelled on both the debate team and the pom-pom squad. She completed her undergraduate degree in symbolic systems and was about to graduate with honors with an MS degree in computer science with an emphasis on artificial intelligence. She was hunting for a job but wasn't really interested in the company called Google that was still in its infancy. In retrospect, she told *Business Week* that she already was acquainted with Stanford PhD students like Larry and Sergey and didn't find working with them an attractive idea because "They love to Rollerblade. They eat pizza for breakfast. They don't shower much. And they don't say 'Sorry' when they bump into you in the hallway."[24]

But after she finished working on a nine-month computer project with 30 other researchers in Switzerland, she received an e-mail from a recruiter about work at Google. She recalled her advisor's enthusiasm about the work Page and Brin were doing. She decided to go for an interview at the small Google office in downtown Palo Alto. After enduring several rigorous interviews, she was impressed by the intelligence of the Google team and what they were trying to accomplish. Marissa took the position of engineer, becoming the first female engineer at Google. Now not only does she influence every new product as well as work to improve existing ones, she also manages 150 product managers. She puts in long days—9 A.M. until midnight. But her hard work has paid off not only in terms of what she has helped Google to accomplish but in terms of personal rewards and recognition as well. With the meteoric growth of the company, she's become a multimillionaire and was recognized by *Newsweek* as one of the 10 Tech Leaders of the Future.

THE GOOGLE TRIUMVIRATE AND CORPORATE STRUCTURE

The section on executive roles in Larry's IPO letter begins with this statement:

> We run Google as a triumvirate. Sergey and I have worked closely together for the last eight years, five at Google. Eric, our CEO, joined Google three years ago. The three of us run the company collaboratively with Sergey and me as Presidents. The structure is unconventional, but we have worked successfully in this way.[25]

He goes on to explain that their collaboration is based on "trust and respect for each other." Although they meet daily, each of them makes decisions unilaterally. Discussion with the larger management team also informs decision making.

Larry notes that Eric Schmidt was hired to provide more business experience. As CEO, Schmidt manages the vice presidents and the sales group. Sergey's area of concentration is engineering and business deals. Larry manages products and also focuses on engineering.

Google's larger management team is organized by function and includes executive management, engineering, products, sales, legal, finance, business operations, and Google.org—its philanthropic branch. Its board of directors has 10 members including Larry, Sergey, and Eric.

Larry explains in his letter the rationale for Google's corporate structure:

We are creating a corporate structure that is designed for stability over long time horizons. By investing in Google, you are placing an unusual long-term bet on the team, especially Sergey and me, and on our innovative approach.[26]

The dual-class ownership structure that went into effect after Google became a publicly owned company allowed Larry and Sergey to remain in control of Google's strategy and culture. They also believe it would enable them to better protect Google's strategy and culture from outside influences. They believed they had developed a management structure, corporate culture, and climate for long-term innovation and growth that would enable Google to meets its mission over time.

Google's Dual-Class Stock

Google has two kinds of stock. When Google went from being a privately owned company to a publicly owned company, it offered prospective shareholders A stock shares, each of which were worth one vote. The B stock shares get 10 votes each and are held by Sergey Brin, Larry Page, and CEO Eric Schmidt. At the time of the initial public offering of Google stock, the three kept one-third of the company's stock, but that gave them about 80% of votes. Although this structure didn't make shareholders happy, dual-class stock made sense to Larry and Sergey. They wanted to retain control of Google to prevent the possibility of a hostile takeover and to have the freedom to steer Google's course in the future. In Google's case, there is no difference between the dividends paid for the two classes of stock, and each would benefit equally if the company were sold.[27]

RECRUITING GOOGLERS

Early in its history, when it was still a privately owned company, Google attracted top talent by offering shares in the company, a unique workplace, and the flexibility and encouragement to the brightest young minds to experiment in their efforts to help Google achieve its noble and challenging mission. They needed engineers who could continue to build the growing network of PCs and to maintain the technical infrastructure that made Google so fast and so efficient. They needed creative engineers to assess users' needs and to conceive of services ahead of the competition. Since many dot-coms were folding during this time, the talent pool for Google was relatively large.

Now, however, Google, Yahoo!, and Microsoft, among others, are engaged in a serious competition for top engineers. Aggressive, systematic, and successful recruiting and hiring are critical to supporting Google's phenomenal growth. According to an online *New York Times* article published in May 2007, in each of the last three years, Google has doubled the number of its employees to a total of over 12,000 worldwide. Currently, Google needs to make about 500 hires per month to support its growth.[28]

Google meets this recruiting challenge in several ways, some of which are traditional and some of which are more creative. One way is to publicize the tangible and intangible benefits of working for Google on its Web site. The top 10 reasons to work at Google posted on the company's Web site are a mix of tangible benefits such as extraordinary workplace comforts and services as well as intangible benefits such as the invitation to join the Google cause, to be a part of "making the world a better place."

Top 10 Reasons to Work at Google

1. *Lend a helping hand.* With millions of visitors every month, Google has become an essential part of everyday life—like a good friend—connecting people with the information they need to live great lives.
2. *Life is beautiful.* Being a part of something that matters and working on products in which you can believe is remarkably fulfilling.
3. *Appreciation is the best motivation,* so we've created a fun and inspiring workspace you'll be glad to be a part of, including on-site doctor and dentist; massage and yoga; professional development opportunities; on-site day care; shoreline running trails; and plenty of snacks to get you through the day.
4. *Work and play are not mutually exclusive.* It is possible to code and pass the puck at the same time.
5. *We love our employees, and we want them to know it.* Google offers a variety of benefits, including a choice of medical programs, company-matched 401(k), stock options, maternity and paternity leave, and much more.
6. *Innovation is our bloodline.* Even the best technology can be improved. We see endless opportunity to create even more relevant, more useful, and faster products for our users. Google is the technology leader in organizing the world's information.
7. *Good company everywhere you look.* Googlers range from former neurosurgeons, CEOs, and U.S. puzzle champions to alligator wrestlers and former-Marines. No matter what their backgrounds Googlers make for interesting cube mates.
8. *Uniting the world, one user at a time.* People in every country and every language use our products. As such we think, act, and work

globally—just our little contribution to making the world a better place.

9. *Boldly go where no one has gone before.* There are hundreds of challenges yet to solve. Your creative ideas matter here and are worth exploring. You'll have the opportunity to develop innovative new products that millions of people will find useful.

10. *There is such a thing as a free lunch after all.* In fact we have them every day: healthy, yummy, and made with love.[29]

John Sullivan, professor and head of human resources at San Francisco State University as well as a human resources advisor to corporations worldwide, offers details about Google recruiting in a July 2006 online article for Australia's online *Human Resources* magazine. Sullivan reports that Google's investment in recruiting surpasses that of "any major product-driven corporation." And he calculates that, "at times, Google recruitment has a ratio of one recruiter for every 14 employees." He says, "If on the surface, this ratio doesn't impress you... compare it to the typically much larger ratio of employees to all HR professionals, which is about 100:1."

He goes on to describe Google's recruiting organization as centralized, staffed by recruitment specialists who have "distinct roles" and "specialized expertise." He comments that "The willingness to fund this recruiting model is a clear indication that talent more than any other input is the most critical at Google, a notion many pay lip service to but few actually execute."[30]

Google's commitment to recruitment is evident in the number and quality of recruiters it employs and the amount of capital it spends to underwrite this part of its organization. Clearly, Google understands that to keep supporting its growth and to keep fueling its think tank, it has to be systematic, thorough, and successful in attracting the very best engineers in the world.

MORE REASONS TO JOIN GOOGLE

Google salaries are kept confidential, but it's safe to assume they are competitive. Furthermore, David Vise reports in a *Washington Post* article that Sergey created multimillion-dollar stock awards to reward teams who produce innovative ideas.[31] This kind of reward in combination with encouragement to pursue individual interests in a workplace that is designed to promote health and happiness is great for existing Googlers and for attracting new talent. Being voted the best company to work for in America two years in a row—a designation that is largely based on the results of a survey given to apparently very happy Googlers—gives recruiting a boost as well.

CREATIVE RECRUITING STRATEGIES

Given the playfulness of Sergey and Larry and the entire Google culture, it's not surprising that Google has unusual strategies in its bag of recruiting tricks. One was to put just an equation followed by dot com—nothing else—on a billboard where commuters between the Silicon Valley and San Francisco would see it. The teasing equation also appeared near Harvard Square on banners at a subway stop. Those who solved the equation and typed the answer into their browsers were given a more difficult problem to solve. Solving this one resulted in an invitation to interview at Google.

Google also hosted the Google Games in 2007 at its Mountain View campus, which featured competitions between computer science and engineering students from Stanford and Berkeley based on video games and complex puzzles. The games provided a way for students to learn about the Google culture while having some fun at the same time. Google also does direct recruiting on about 200 college campuses nationwide.

Google Code Jam is a contest that Google has sponsored in the United States, Europe, Latin America, China, and India to reach the software engineer community worldwide. Winners are awarded cash prizes, and Google has a chance to look at the talent that participates for possible recruiting. The contest is a big draw. Code Jam Europe attracted 10,000 registrants from 15 different countries in 2006. Aside from recruiting benefits, it's good PR, and it is one more way that Google builds it community.

GETTING HIRED BY GOOGLE

Google's Web site provides clear information about the rigorous hiring process. After submitting an application, applicants will be contacted by the recruiting team. A 30 to 40-minute phone interview conducted by someone in a role similar to the one for which you've applied is next. The purpose of this interview is to determine whether an applicant's technical skills are sufficient to warrant a face-to-face interview.

The live interview will consist of talking to at least four different interviewers. Several engineers will assess the applicant's skills, which includes solving problems while on site. You'll also talk to managers. You are "hired by a committee," not by an individual. Tips for the interview offered on its Web site include learning about Google's products and services before the interview, practicing solving problems at TopCoder.com, the outfit that helps it with its Code Jam competitions, and reflecting on what interests you about Google.

Whether to hire an individual is so important to Google that it may take up to two weeks to make the decision. Perhaps the most noteworthy characteristic of the process is the extent to which it involves a committee of Googlers, not just human resource personnel and managers.

By early 2007, Google was receiving 100,000 job applications each month. Because of that incredible volume of applications to process and the importance Google attaches to its workplace culture and finding people who will not only fit in, but flourish, in its environment, it has developed an extensive online questionnaire for applicants to help them determine whether an applicant is a good fit for the Google culture. Google is proud of the fact that only 4% of its workforce leaves each year—less than other tech companies in the Silicon Valley. Losing and replacing employees is expensive and it slows production, so making the best possible hiring decisions is a smart strategy.

Google's rigorous hiring practices have helped to ensure that it brings new employees into the Google fold who are not only highly qualified to make a contribution to Google's product development and service but also that they will be a good fit for the Google culture.

The quality of the search results and other Google tools and services attracts a huge global audience of users, which, in turn, attracts advertising dollars. The enterprise products and services it markets generate more revenue. Google needs bright, energetic, innovative, and dedicated engineers to form the think tank to produce new products and services and to enhance and refine existing ones. Larry and Sergey justifiably refer to the Googlers as the company's most important asset and, to honor that fact, they have created a corporate culture to attract and keep the best.

NOTES

1. "Getting into Google: Hiring Process," Google Jobs, http://www. google. com/support/jobs/bin/static.py?page=gettingintogoogle.html&sid=hiringprocess (accessed February 16, 2008).

2. http://money.cnn.com/galleries/2007/fortune/0701/gallery.Google_life/ (accessed January 27, 2008).

3. "Fortune: 100 Best Companies to Work For," CNN Money.com, http:// money.cnn.com/element/ssi/sections/mag/fortune/bestcompanies/2007/box_ how.popup.html (accessed February 20, 2008).

4. Larry Page and Sergey Brin, "Letter from the Founders: 'An Owner's Manual' for Google's Shareholders," Google Investor Relations, http://investor. google.com/ipo_letter.html (accessed April 12, 2008).

5. "Company Overview," Google Corporate Information, http://www.google. com/corporate/ (accessed March 28, 2008).

6. "Our Philosophy," Google Corporate Information, http://www.google. com/corporate/tenthings.html (accessed April 12, 2008).

7. http://www.sec.gov/Archives/edgar/data/1288776/000119312504139655/ ds1a.htm#toc59330_25b (accessed March 7, 2008).

8. Vikram Khanna, "The Voice of Google; CEO Eric Schmidt Talks to Vikram Khanna about What Powers the Search Engine Icon," *Business Times Singapore,* January 12, 2008 (found on LexisNexis).

9. "Google Code of Conduct," Google Investor Relations, http://investor. google.com/conduct.html (accessed April 10, 2008).

10. Elinor Mills, "Newsmaker: Meet Google's Culture Czar," CNET News. com, April 27, 2007, http://www.news.com/Meet-Googles-culture-czar/2008-1023_3-6179897.html (accessed February 18, 2008).

11. Sheridan Prasso, "Google Goes to India," *Fortune,* October 23, 2007, http:// money.cnn.com/2007/10/18/news/international/google_india.fortune/index. htm (accessed April 27, 2008).

12. Elinor Mills, "Newsmaker: Meet Google's Culture Czar," CNET News. com, April 27, 2007, http://www.news.com/Meet-Googles-culture-czar/2008-1023_3-6179897.html (accessed January 30, 2008).

13. Charlie Ayers, http://www.chefcharlieayers.com/(accessed June 26, 2008).

14. John Cloud, "Eating Better than Organic," *Time,* March 2, 2007, http:// www.time.com/time/magazine/article/0,9171,1595245-4,00.html (accessed May 25, 2008).

15. Olivia Wu, "Now Google's Cooking" SF Gate, March 1, 2006, http:// www.sfgate.com/cgi-bin/article.cgi?f=/chronicle/archive/2006/03/01/FDG 32H9OF61.DTL (accessed May 26, 2008).

16. Diane McClamroch, "Growing Our Connection to Food, The Official Google Blog," May 9, 2008, http://googleblog.blogspot.com/search/label/inno vation (accessed May 26, 2008).

17. The Growing Connection, http://www.thegrowingconnection.org (accessed May 28, 2008).

18. Larry Page and Sergey Brin, "Letter from the Founders: An Owner's Manual for Google Shareholders, Google Investor Relations," http://investor.google. com/ipo_letter.html (accessed April 4, 2008).

19. Sara Kehaulani Goo, "Building a 'Googley' Workforce," *The Washington Post,* October 21, 2006 http://www.washingtonpost.com/wpdyn/content/ article/2006/10/20/AR2006102001461_2.html (accessed April 7, 2008).

20. "Benefits," Google Jobs, http://www.google.com/support/jobs/bin/static. py?page=benefits.html (accessed February 16, 2008).

21. Arie de Geus, "The living company," *Harvard Business Review*, Vol. 75 No. 2, 58.

22. http://www.sec.gov/Archives/edgar/data/1288776/000119312504139655/ ds1a.htm#toc59330_25b (accessed March 28, 2008).

23. Vikram Khanna, "The Voice of Google, CEO Eric Schmidt Talks to Vikram Khanna about What Powers the Search Engine Icon," *Business Times,* Singapore, January 12, 2008 (found on LexisNexis, accessed April 10, 2008).

24. "Managing Google's Idea Factory: Marissa Mayer Helps the Search Giant Out-Think Its Rivals," *BusinessWeek,* October 3, 2005, http://www.businessweek. com/magazine/content/05_40/b3953093.htm (accessed April 15, 2008).

25. Larry Page and Sergey Brin, "Letter from the Founders: An Owner's Manual for Google Shareholders, Google Investor Relations," http://investor.google. com/ipo_letter.html (accessed March 7, 2008).

26. Ibid.

27. Thomas Eisenmann, "Betting on Google's Future," *Wall Street Journal,* August 24, 2004, http://online.wsj.com/article/SB109330251535299069.html?mod=COLUMN (accessed April 16, 2008).

28. Miguel Helft, "In Fierce Competition, Google Finds Novel Ways to Feed Hiring Machine," *New York Times,* May 28, 2007, http://www.nytimes.com/2007/05/28/technology/28recruit.html?_r=2&sq=In%20Fierce%20Competition,%20Google%20Finds%20Novel%20Ways%20to%20Feed%20Hiring%20Machine&st=nyt&adxnnl=1&oref=slogin&scp=1&adxnnlx=1203831135-1aUfJ5Z8W0C-1QWFE3kEpTA (accessed April 5, 2008).

29. "Top 10 Reasons to Work at Google," Google Jobs, http://www.google.com/support/jobs/bin/static.py?page=about.html&about=top10 (accessed February 18, 2008).

30. John Sullivan, "A Look Inside the Google Talent Machine," Human Resources, July 25, 2006, http://www.humanresourcesmagazine.com.au/articles/B1/0C0429B1.asp?Type=60&Category=1223 (accessed February 12, 2008).

31. David Vise, "What Lurks in Its Soul?," *Washington Post,* November 13, 2005, http://www.washingtonpost.com/wpdyn/content/article/2005/11/11/AR2005111101644.html (accessed April 2, 2008).

Chapter Six

How Google Uses Fun to Attract Customers

Google uses fun to draw people to its site. High traffic to the site helps it attract more advertising dollars. But it seems that Googlers are also genuinely interested in having fun.

Of course, having fun with Google depends on one's definition of fun. But Google has something for everyone. Along with the fun, often there's an opportunity to learn as well. Some of the free tools we'll consider also have enterprise editions.

Larry and Sergey and the Googlers are committed to excellent service to those who use Google and to research to develop new products and services. But they also like to have fun in the workplace. This is evident in the exercise balls, lava lamps, electric scooters, game rooms, and dogs that share their work space and the weekly hockey games on skates in the Googleplex parking lot, among other things. They also share this sense of fun with the world in various ways. We'll look at some of those ways and also look at how to have fun—and be more productive and maybe even increase sales and profits—with some of the Google tools.

GOOGLE DOODLES

For those of us who use Google search a lot, it's always a treat to open the Google home page to find a Google doodle. A Google doodle is artwork around the Google logo that is usually, on a day-to-day basis, the word *Google*. The colors of the letters in the order in which they appear are blue, red, orange, blue, green, and red. Google doodles appear on holidays, sometimes in response to current events, and sometimes in honor of an historical event.

Dennis Hwang is the artist behind the Google doodles. He is also the Google international Web master who manages the international site content. While the first doodle was the creation of Larry and Sergey, Dennis has created over 100 Google doodles since 2000. He started as an intern with Google while he was in college. Larry and Sergey were fascinated with the idea of holiday logos before he came on the scene. When he joined Google, they figured since he had also been studying art, they'd ask him to create some holiday logos. Dennis says on his blog that he's been doing them ever since as his 20% project, and it's the favorite part of his job.

> Holding up my mockups and then holding my breath while Larry and Sergey do their "thumbs-up, thumbs-down" emperor thing is never boring, and I love the fact that my little niche within this company turned out to be something so cool and creative and, well, Google-y.[1]

Dennis starts his creative process by brainstorming. Then he searches for images using Google Images. Once he's saturated with images, he starts to work on a doodle with his favorite design approach of having images or the additional artwork of the doodle interact with the letters that spell Google. He says that he puts more effort into one of his favorite topics—artists' birthdays.

Dennis welcomes suggestions for Google doodles. He has to come up with new ideas every year for the same holidays. He explains the challenge on his blog when he says, "There's only so many ways to draw a turkey or a pumpkin!"[2] Dennis does get a lot of suggestions, because Google has established that it is truly open to suggestions and finds that they contribute to the creativity from which doodles are born.

Dennis gets lots of ideas from K–12 students who are invited on the Google Web site to join in the Doodle 4 Google contests that run every year. Google announces a particular theme and challenges kids to create a Google doodle around that them. In 2008, the theme is "What if…?"

On its Web site, Google offers teachers lesson plans that will help theme integrate the competition with their curricula.

APRIL FOOL'S DAY PRANKS

In 2000, Google introduced the Mentalplex. To log into Mentalplex, users were instructed to first remove hats and glasses. Then they were told to look into the swirling red and blue circle with the emphatic all capital letters directive to not move their heads. Then they were told to "project mental image" of what they wanted to find. And, finally, they were to click or "visualize clicking" within the swirling MentalPlex circle. It was a great spoof because everyone would most likely think that an actual search process like this would be great and also it didn't seem that far out of the realm of possibilities that Google might be able to create and provide the service free to users.

Mentalplex comes complete with FAQs that include these troubleshooting tips:

> *Problem:* MentalPlex keeps taking me to sites featuring rubber toys, nipples and diapering.

Answer: Your infant is too close to the monitor. If you have no
   children, you may want to consider counseling.

Problem: I am unable to visualize clicking and have to use my finger
   to activate the mouse.

Answer: Click visualization takes practice. Try pushing the mouse
   button with your eyebrow, then gradually increase the distance
   between your eye and the mouse.

Problem: I have a clear picture of what I want, but no results are
   returned.

Answer: The object you desire may not be found on the web. If you
   are looking for the current location of Atlantis, Amelia Earhart or
   your car keys, MentalPlex may not be able to help you.[3]

On April 1, 2002, Google revealed the secret behind their search engine's speed and accuracy was a system for ranking pages called Pigeon-
Rank. Larry and Sergey found that "low cost pigeon clusters" (PCs) could
determine the relevancy of Web pages faster than humans or machines.
The Web page revealing this system on the site noted:

By collecting flocks of pigeons in dense clusters, Google is able
to process search queries at speeds superior to traditional search
engines, which typically rely on birds of prey, brooding hens or
slow-moving waterfowl to do their relevance rankings.[4]

It was a grand spoof on itself complete with data and diagrams and
FAQs. Full of rich and hilarious detail, you can imagine how much fun
it was for Google to dream up and to present. It's certainly fun to read.
In this paragraph, Google explains how PigeonRank works. It's actually
a simplified explanation of PageRank except...well...for the pigeons.

When a search query is submitted to Google, it is routed to a data
coop where monitors flash result pages at blazing speeds. When a
relevant result is observed by one of the pigeons in the cluster, it
strikes a rubber-coated steel bar with its beak, which assigns the
page a PigeonRank value of one. For each peck, the PigeonRank
increases. Those pages receiving the most pecks, are returned at
the top of the user's results page with the other results displayed
in pecking order.[5]

PigeonRank has the integrity users have come to expect from Google.
We are assured that "pigeon-driven methods make tampering" with results
difficult. Even if a Web site tries to increase its ranking by including images
of food that might encourage an unwarranted peck, the pigeons are not
deceived.

In 2004, we learned that the Google Copernicus Center, a lunar hosting and research center, was hiring. It seemed like this might actually be in the realm of possibilities for Google. Anything is possible, right?

The Google Copernicus Hosting Environment and Experiment in Search Engineering (G.C.H.E.E.S.E.) is a fully integrated research, development and technology facility at which Google will be conducting experiments in entropized information filtering, high-density high-delivery hosting (HiDeHiDeHo) and de-oxygenated cubicle dwelling.[6]

And we discovered that we'd been very nearly taken for a ride again.

But that same day, Google announced that it was testing a free Web-mail service called Gmail with the unprecedented free storage capacity of up to one gigabyte, which was over 100 times what was being offered by competitors. Larry casually explained in the press release that they had developed and were testing this service in response to a Google user's complaints about the weaknesses and annoyances of current e-mail programs. Cynical media and savvy Google users wrote this off as another Google April Fool's prank. In fact, it was for real.

Google Gulp was introduced in 2005, designed to increase the intelligence of Google users and thereby optimize their use of the Google search engine. Google was laughing at itself and its initial offering of Gmail by invitation only when they explained how to get Google Gulp:

How to Get Gulped?

You can pick up your own supply of this "limited release" product simply by turning in a used Gulp Cap at your local grocery store. How to get a Gulp Cap? Well, if you know someone who's already been "gulped," they can give you one. And if you don't know anyone who can give you one, don't worry—that just means you aren't cool. But very, very (very!) soon, you will be.[7]

April 1, 2006, gave us Google Romance, which parodies online dating services. In a press release entitled "Google to Organize World's Courtship Information with Google Romance," we learned that Google Romance offered "users both a psychographic matchmaking service and all-expenses-paid dates for couples who agree to experience contextually relevant advertising throughout the course of their evening." Jonathan Rosenberg, Google's senior vice president of product management, commented in the press release, "let's face it: in what area of life is the world's information more disorganized than romance? We thought we could use our search technology to help you find that special someone, then send you on a date and use contextual ads to help you, ya know—close the deal." When we clicked to learn more, we noted that, in the case study presented about User A and User B's date, the personal contextual ads they listened to during their dinner were based on their dating histories. The "persistent drone" of the subliminal ads influenced their dating conversation and led them to the conclusion that they were socioeconomically compatible.[8]

On the eve of April Fool's Day, 2007, a new service called Gmail Paper was introduced on the login page for Gmail, Google's free e-mail service. Google would print however many copies of each e-mail a user requested. Google would ship a potentially mammoth paper archive to the user free as long as the user understood that each printed e-mail copy would have, to offset the cost of postage, a relevant advertisement printed in bold red 36-point type. The user was assured that there would be no pop-up ads or animations because these were not an option in the paper medium. Not to worry about wasting trees; Gmail Paper actually brought incremental improvement to the environment since "Gmail Paper is made out of 96% post-consumer organic soybean sputum."[9]

As if Gmail Paper wasn't enough, the next day, April 1, 2007, Google announced free in-home wireless broadband service that offered "self-installed plumbing-based Internet access." Those of us still stuck in the backwoods without high-speed Internet wondered wistfully whether they would soon develop a system that would work in septic systems and not just municipal sewage systems.

The Toilet Internet Service Provider (TiSP) project was described as a "self-installed, ad-supported online service that will be offered entirely free to any consumer with a WiFi-capable PC and a toilet connected to a local municipal sewage system." Larry told the world in the press release:

> "We've got that whole organizing-the-world's-information thing more or less under control," said Google Co-founder and President Larry Page, a longtime supporter of so-called "dark porcelain" research and development. "What's interesting, though, is how many different modalities there are for actually getting that information to you—not to mention from you."[10]

The TiSP web page has step-by-step photos to show just how easy the installation is. But professional installation is also available. This service "dispatches an army of factory-trained, sub-contracted nanobots from the TiSP Access Node. The nanobots travel with exhilarating nano-speed through the sewer system and into your home to perform the installation service, which should be complete within 15 minutes."[11]

April Fool's Day is a widely anticipated holiday for Google users. You just never know what the Googlers are going to think up next to make us laugh on this goofy holiday.

GOOGLE LUNAR X PRIZE

For those who are fascinated by space exploration, watching what happens in response to Google offering its $30 million Google Lunar X Prize (www.googlelunarxprize.org) should be fun. It's an international competition that, to win, requires safely landing a robot on the moon. The robot then has to cruise 500 meters on the moon's surface and send images and data back to earth. To compete, you'll need to be 90% privately funded and must register by December 31, 2010. The first team that lands and completes the competition's mission will receive $20 million. The second place team will receive $15 million. The remaining $5 million will be used for bonus prizes.

Sergey's enthusiasm about the competition was evident in his comments reported in a *New York Times* article: "The idea we can help spur the return to the moon and maybe even do it more quickly than some of the national plans is really exciting to me."[12] Sergey also commented that Google's underwriting of the competition might be compared with the way some companies sponsor yacht races.

MAKING AND KEEPING FRIENDS

Orkut (orkut.com), introduced in January 2004, is Google's social networking tool. It was named after Orkut Buyukkokten, a Google engineer who developed it in his 20% time at Google—the time Google requires its engineers to work on what interests them. It's a way to keep in touch with current friends and family by posting messages, photos, and videos. It can also be used as a way to meet new people who share your interests. There are lots of online communities within orkut that discuss a wide range of topics such as current events, and any member can start a community. Orkut has grown by leaps and bounds. It now has over 100 million users. Orkut was initially designed for the United States market, but it turned out to be extremely popular in Brazil and India. It is the most frequently visited Web site in India and the second most popular site in Brazil. As of March 2008, almost 70% of the traffic to orkut is from Brazil, while 15% comes from India.

GOOGLE VIDEO

Google's Video's index (www.video.google.com) is the most comprehensive on the Web. Viewers can search a collection of millions of indexed videos that include movie clips, documentaries, amateur productions, TV shows, music videos from Google's YouTube, Google Video, and other third-party sites. Google puts the best search engine in the world to work not only searching those sources but also crawling billions of pages from all over the Web to find relevant videos that match your search terms.

Google's ongoing commitment to video continued with its acquisition of YouTube in 2006, just a year after YouTube was officially launched. In its short life, YouTube quickly became the premier destination for users to share and view original videos globally on the Web. It also allows people to share video a variety of ways—via Web sites, blogs, e-mail, and mobile devices. Just as blogs enabled everyone to share their thoughts in print, YouTube empowers people to become video producers and to make their movies, whether informational or creative, available to the world. YouTube also has partnerships with professional producers of video such as CBS, the BBC, and Warner Music Group. Hundreds of millions of videos are viewed daily online on its site. According to Nielsen//NetRatings of December 2007, YouTube is the number one entertainment site on the Internet, and it has the sixth largest audience on the Internet.

SHOPPING

Some people enjoy the ease of shopping online. Google makes shopping easy with a shopping link right on the top of its home page. Clicking on this link takes you to Google Product Search, which is currently in Beta.

In Beta

To designate a service or technology tool as being "in Beta" means that it is still being tested. Implicitly, if not explicitly, the provider of a beta product is asking that users be patient and forgiving if it doesn't work right. The company is still working out the kinks. Often, companies invite users to provide feedback on their product, tool, or service to get help working out the kinks. The term has lost some of its meaning either because new offerings seem to stay in Beta for years or they leave Beta with few improvements or enhancement.

Once you've registered for free with Google to use Product Search, some shopping tools are available that make it possible to create and share your shopping list; make notes about products of interest; and sort products by item, date, and price. Google claims to have the largest collection of products and merchants on the Web. The results it provides are unbiased in that Google does not sell places in its search results to merchants. Any advertising is clearly designated as a sponsored link. So the search results returned are based on the Google search engine's attempt to give you the most relevant products based on your query.

Google Product Search started its life at Google with the name of Froogle, which was a pun on the word *frugal*. But Google decided to change the name in 2007 because it didn't seem to clearly indicate what the product does. Google Checkout was a feature added to make buying fast and secure.

GOOGLE SKETCHUP

If three-dimensional modeling appeals to you, the free Google SketchUp software tool (www.sketchup.google.com) might be the Google toy for you. Maybe you want to remodel your kitchen and see how it will look in 3-D. If you're a local history buff, you could reconstruct that eighteenth-century courthouse that was destroyed by fire. For the avid gardener, SketchUp could help you render a new landscape plan before you put your shovel in the dirt. To plan a country getaway on that new piece of land you bought, use SketchUp to help with the 3-D model and then use Google Earth to place it on the satellite image of your new land to see how it might look.

BLOGGING AND CREATING A WEB PAGE

Do you want to publish a page on the Web so that others can read it and respond to it? Then maybe you'd get a kick out of starting a blog. Blogger (www.blogger.com) was started by three friends as a small company called Pyra Labs in 1999. Google bought the company in 2002. On its Web site, Blogger founders comment on life after becoming part of Google: "Now we're a small (but slightly bigger than before) team in Google focusing on helping people have their own voice on the web and organizing the world's information from the personal perspective. Which has pretty much always been our whole deal."[13]

Starting a blog on Blogger requires registering for a free Google account. It's easy to start your own blog, and there are thousands of other blogs to read and respond to as well.

With the same free Google account, you can also create a Web page to share your thoughts, images, and video snippets with others. Google Page Creator is a Google Labs project, which means it's still being tested, and Google Labs welcomes suggestions and comments on people's experiences with this tool. It doesn't require any special skills or knowledge of HTML to use this tool to create your Web page.

Blogs

Blogs got their start as sites that offered alternative viewpoints on different subjects, including the news. The word *blog* is a shortened version of *Web log,* and it is used as a noun as in "check out my blog" and as a verb as in "I'm going to blog about my views on two presidential candidates." Easy-to-use tools like Blogger opened the door for millions of people to become journalists and commentators as well as to blog for recreation. Blogs can include images and links to other blogs and Web sites. Because readers of blogs can leave comments, blogs can become highly interactive.

By December 2007, Technorati, a search engine devoted to blogs, was tracking more than 100 million blogs.

Blogging has influenced mainstream media by sometimes bringing new information to the public's attention, which has forced the mainstream to focus on a particular issue as well. By 2004, blogs became commonplace as bloggers provided almost instantaneous commentary on breaking news, political candidates, business, and entertainment. Political candidates and news media jumped on board, using blogs to reach the public.[14]

GOOGLE LABS

If you like trying out new Web-based tools before all the kinks are worked out of them, Google Labs (www.labs.google.com) is the place to explore. It's the part of Google's Web site where researchers and software engineers invite the public to look at new projects and to provide feedback. Some of the projects never get into full development. But others, like Google Docs and Spreadsheets, Google Maps, Google Video, and Google News Alerts "graduated" from Google Labs to become permanent offerings to the public for its use. In the Lab FAQs, users are asked to be patient "if a demo refuses to run, or even walk quickly" because some of them receive only spare-time support from engineers. Google makes it clear that they welcome developing projects interactively with users when they state: "If you have something to say about a Google Labs product, we can't encourage you strongly enough to e-mail us your ideas, comments, suggestions and tales of woe, or post them on the discussion group for the particular demo you're referencing."[15]

THE JOY OF PURE SEARCH

For many people, just searching for answers to questions quickly or finding an array of information on a topic of interest is joyful using Google. Have a few lines from a song running through your head but you can't remember the band or the name of the song? Just type in the lines in the Google search box. Are you anxious to get going on planting your early spring vegetables but aren't sure if it's too early? Find the information you need quickly on Google.

News buffs can click on the news link on the Google home page and access headlines from more than 4,500 English-language worldwide news sources. Links are provided to several articles on every news story so that you can read different versions of the same breaking news story from different publishers. You also have the option to create personalized news that will show you stories that best correspond with your interests. Users can receive news alerts on topics of interest, and news can be accessed via mobile phone. The history buff can search historical news archives that go back over 200 years.

The instant gratification that we all experience when we find an answer or information quickly on Google is a joy that we could come to take for granted. To avoid that, just remember what life would be like if we couldn't Google to find fast, relevant search results.

GOOGLE EARTH

We've all seen the stunning pictures of earth taken from space. Even in our mind's eye, it's hard to imagine all the cities and towns and wild spaces or think of all the people all over the planet. But we can pretend we're visitors from a faraway galaxy and use Google Earth (www.earth. google.com) to explore.

Google Earth, first released in 2005, uses a combination of satellite imagery, aerial photography, and geographical information systems to let explorers wander the globe from the comfort of their desktops. It has a very simple interface that lets users point and zoom to anywhere on the globe. If you want an exact point, you can type in an address nearly anywhere on earth and let Google Earth take you there.

Try this. Put in your address and Google Earth will fly over the earth, zoom in to a decent height, and hover over you. Maybe you're more interested in seeing where someone else lives. The Google Earth database is huge so that, chances are, no matter what you type in, you'll find it. How about the Aran Islands of Ireland? Type it into the "Fly to" box and watch as Google Earth takes you there. If you have a relative you'd like to visit who lives there, it will even give you detailed directions.

Google layers are another feature of Google Earth that let users do everything from flying along at ground level to get a feel for the terrain to a 3-D view of the hills and rivers in the countryside or the buildings and streets in a city. Informational layers tied to Wikipedia, Panoramio, and community members all over the world provide information and interesting facts about the places you decide to visit. Featured content layers display information provided by National Geographic, NASA, the United Nations, and the Discovery Channel, to name a few. Here you'll find all the science and history of a place. You'll even find reviews of the restaurants there. A really fun one is the Rumsey Historical Maps layer. You can see what London looked like in Victorian times or see what a globe in 1790 would have looked like.

A site called Google Earth Blog (www.gearthblog.com), which is not an official Google blog, has lots of news about Google Earth and how people are using it. It offers good tips to beginners and more experienced users of Google Earth. The Google Earth Community on this site holds discussions among a host of like-minded explorers in the forum. Google also has a Google Earth blog that is active on its site when it wants to note a new feature or a newsworthy event around this tool.

Google Earth is such a fascinating tool that it pulls thousands of visitors from all over the world to the Google site. It grew out of Google's acquisition of the company Keyhole, and it turned out to be a smart acquisition for it not only to build traffic to the site but because it could then develop an enterprise edition based on it for governments and corporations.

The U.S. Forest Service purchased the enterprise edition to assist its employees and other government employees in fighting fires. Dell uses the enterprise version to visualize its global Web site traffic, which has strengthened the sense of community with its partners. Dell's global Enterprise Command Center provides it with a global view of customer activity at a glance, giving Dell the means to respond efficiently to customers.

The Alabama Department of Homeland Security's (DHS) model of how it used the Google Earth enterprise edition is interesting and suggests how the market for this Google product is wide open and could be used in any other state in the United States as well as other countries to support security and emergency response programs. The ability to create a secure system with Google Earth Enterprise promoted buy-in by the contributing organizations and groups that needed to contribute information to the Alabama DHS's program to make it work. Furthermore, by using a common platform, duplication of effort by different agencies was eliminated, which also reduced costs.

Chris Johnson, vice president of geospatial technologies at GTAC at the U.S. Space and Rocket Center, which has been instrumental in helping with implementation of the homeland security project, explained that its usability makes "Google Earth Enterprise...a keystone to this program....We call it a twelve-year-old program," she explains, "because any twelve-year-old could use it."[16]

Alabama has been able to use Google Earth Enterprise to create a valuable common operational picture for emergency personnel across the state. The state uses it to plan emergency evacuation routing, critical infrastructure mapping, visualization of risks, and to create effective disaster response scenarios, among other things. Google Earth Enterprise helped Alabama reach the next level in emergency preparedness and response to man-made or natural disasters.

Google Earth in Practice

I e-mailed a friend and colleague, Tim Cannon, a media specialist, to ask whether he used Google Earth and what he thought about it. Tim is an Englishman who lives in the United States with his American wife, Rebecca, two corgis, and a pack of felines, but his family and many friends still live in England. This is how he replied.

> Google Earth—without it, my world would be a lot smaller and a lot less interesting. Having Google Earth on my computer feels like having your own satellite, ready to zip around the

globe at any time of the day or night, to seek out even the most remote parts of the globe just for me. I see it as a great supplement to my life, a tool to enhance my knowledge of the world and just a great addition to my already curious nature.

For instance, I moved to America from England about twenty years ago and, even though I get to travel back there fairly often, sometimes there's no resisting the still strong siren call of my native country. With Google Earth, I can go for a quick fly over my old hometown, or take a quick spin over what I still think as some of the most beautiful landscapes in the world. Sometimes I yearn for the wilds of North Wales or the Scottish Highlands, places I have spent a lot of time in, and although Google Earth can't, yet, replicate the experience of being there, it can do everything but. It'll take you to Fort William in Scotland or Porthmadog in Wales, show you the mountains and the heather or grass on the mountains, or the streams and the lochs they run into; it'll show photos and point out details you had forgotten; at which point, I find, the memories take over and I'm almost there . . . but drier and warmer.

It has other uses for me, too, of course. Recently my brother moved to Yorkshire. He sent me photos but I always like to situate things in their environment. I want to see the area in which he lives, the nearest city, where he walks his dogs. So I go to Google Earth and find his new town. . . . and see what a great place he's moved to. His house backs up to the Yorkshire Dales, a great place to go walking, and looks out over a small old English town, dominated by an old ruined Castle, and look, there's the train station with trains to the nearest city, Newcastle. Looks fantastic, how great it would be to visit! And should I wish to, by clicking on the train station, of course, I can book a ticket to get there.

Other times I'll use Google Earth as a way of enriching books I'm reading. Right now, for instance, I'm reading a travel book about Europe in which the author visited all the historical "hotspots" at the turn of the millennium to note the dramatic changes Europe had experienced over the course of the last century. One of the early chapters concerned itself with the First World War, something that resonated with me because when I was a child I remember my Grandfather talking of his experiences in many of the places that the author visited. The author visits Ypres, the site of one of the biggest battles of the War, and I can still vividly remember my Grandfather's reminiscences about being there, and so, Google Earth to hand, I follow both the author's and my

Grandfather's marches around Belgium and Northern France. Google Earth is at its very best here for it not only shows the actual sites but also links to photos and Wikipedia entries. Suddenly, I find that my experience of the book has been enriched tenfold. By seeing these places in Google Earth, by virtually travelling there, to Ypres, Verdun, and the Somme, I am drawn in to the book and nearer to my Grandfather. And that's just one of the chapters of one particular book; Google Earth has served me well through many books.

I use it the same way for current affairs and magazine articles and papers and projects, providing a way of expanding my view of what's going on around the world. I can follow the demonstrations in Tibet by using Google Earth to show me not only Lhasa, the capital, but also some of the lesser known protest sites, Gansu, for instance. Then, by clicking on links generated by other users, I can look at photos of the monasteries that have also been involved in protests. Suddenly the news is not something that happens to other people but something that I realise that I am involved in. Google Earth makes me realise how we're all connected. I'll see something on the news, in a book or magazine, or remember a place I used to go to as a kid, turn on Google Earth and go there. Maybe Google Earth has turned us all into potential explorers. I could go on, but Google Earth is waiting and there is much to see!

Google seems like a testimonial to the notion that it's possible to have fun at work and to make money at the same time. Enamored as they are with both coding and roller-blading, Googlers state in their top ten reasons to work for Google: "Work and play are not mutually exclusive. It is possible to code and pass the puck at the same time."[17]

Google has helped to build its global community with Google users by offering snippets of humor on its Web site as well as tools for having fun. This same community is a potential audience for the advertising that generates the majority of Google's income. So we might say that it's possible to have fun and make money at the same time without doing any harm. Looked at another way, creating all those tools and fun ways to play is also marketing money wisely spent.

What does Google do with its money besides put it back into the business? Google, always different, uses some of its money to support its own unusual brand of philanthropy. We'll explore how Google lives up to the implicit half of its motto that requires it to not only not be evil, but to do good as well.

NOTES

1. Dennis Hwang, "Oodles of Doodles," The Official Google Blog, June 8, 2004, http://googleblog.blogspot.com/2004/06/oodles-of-doodles.html (accessed March 6, 2008).

2. Ibid.

3. "Google MentalPlex Frequently Asked Questions," Google: How to Google, http://www.google.com/mentalplex/MP_faq.html (accessed March 9, 2008).

4. "Our Search: Google Technology," Google, http://www.google.com/technology/pigeonrank.html (accessed March 10, 2008).

5. Ibid.

6. "Google Copernicus Center Is Hiring," Google Job Opportunities, http://www.google.com/jobs/lunar_job.html (accessed March 10, 2008).

7. "Quench Your Thirst for Knowledge," Google Gulp, http://www.google.com/googlegulp (accessed March 6, 2008).

8. Google Romance, http://www.google.com/romance/tour.html (accessed March 11, 2008).

9. "About Gmail Paper," http://mail.google.com/mail/help/paper/more.html (accessed March 11, 2008).

10. "Google Provides Free In-Home Wireless Broadband Service," http://www.google.com/tisp/press.html.

11. "TiSP: Going with the Flow," Google TiSP, http://www.google.com/tisp/install.html (accessed March 9, 2008).

12. Brad Stone, "A Google Competition, With a Robotic Moon Landing as a Goal," *New York Times*, February 22, 2008, http://www.nytimes.com/2008/02/22/business/22space.html?_r=1&oref=slogin (accessed April 29, 2008).

13. "The Story of Blogger," http://www.blogger.com/about (accessed March 7, 2008).

14. "blog," http://www.techweb.com/encyclopedia/defineterm.jhtml?term=BLOG (accessed March 6, 2008).

15. "Google Labs: Frequently Asked Questions," http://labs.google.com/faq.html (accessed March 10, 2008).

16. "Alabama Department of Homeland Security," Google Earth, http://earth.google.com/enterprise/virtual_alabama.html (accessed March 11, 2008).

17. "Top 10 Reasons To Work at Google," Google Jobs, http://www.google.com/support/jobs/bin/static.py?page=about.html&about=top10 (accessed April 4, 2008).

Chapter Seven

Google Philanthropy

Google's reach spans the globe, yet our hope is that by aggressively applying our resources to address the world's most significant social problems, Google.org [Google's philanthropic arm] will one day surpass the parent company's worldwide influence. We have a deep passion to find innovative solutions and entrepreneurial approaches to such issues as global poverty, climate change and global public health.[1]

Larry and Sergey started Google with the unique vision of making the best search engine in the world to make all the information in the world available to everyone. They created one of the richest companies in the world based on this vision by connecting the most relevant search results for a query with the most relevant targeted ads related to a specific search. It's not surprising that their unique vision, the human and technology resources at Google, the company's wealth, and their social philosophy would result in an innovative approach to philanthropy.

Larry and Sergey outlined their philanthropic vision as early as 2004 in their letter to prospective shareholders at the time of their initial public offering. Early in the formation of Google.org, Google created a fund worth the value of 10% of the 3 million shares from Google's initial public stock offering. This fund was used to establish the tax-exempt Google Foundation in 2005. The Google Foundation is a separate 501(c)(3) private foundation. Google.org manages the Google Foundation. The Google Foundation supports the mission and core initiatives of Google.org. However, the Foundation is only one source of funds used by Google.org for grant making and investments. As of January 2008, Google.org's giving and investments totaled over $75 million.[2]

Larry and Sergey's decision to make Google.org a "hybrid philanthropy" that combines donations through grants and investments for profit may seem odd, but, in fact, it gives them more options and more latitude as they search for solutions for complex global problems. It also gives them the opportunity to make a return on their investment in companies they partner with, if together they find solutions that have high market value. If they do make profits from their investments in for-profit companies, the money would be put back into Google.org to support additional Google.org activities.[3]

The flexibility Google.org gains from being a for-profit organization can really help it attempt to develop solutions in different ways. For example, as it seeks to promote development of better plug-in hybrid electric vehicles, it was able to award $1 million in grants to nonprofit organizations such as Plug-In America and CalCars that will campaign to raise public awareness about plug-in cars. But it was also able to issue a request for proposals for $10 million in investments that has the potential to stimulate companies to develop solutions. They want to be in the position to find the best solution whether that solution will come from grants to nonprofit organizations or for-profit organizations or some combination. Structured in this manner, Google.org can also lobby the government about issues of concern.

Larry and Sergey wanted to create a philanthropic organization that would address some of the most serious global challenges of the new millennium. But they also wanted to select causes that would be a good match with Google's strengths of information retrieval and technology to become directly involved in problem solving. Those strengths, in combination with the expertise and knowledge of those with whom they might partner, could create powerful responses to formidable social problems. Google selected climate change, poverty, and emerging disease as its challenges. It believes that climate change, global health, and poverty are "inextricably interrelated and it is the poor of the world who bear the heaviest burden" of their effects. With Google.org, the company wants to fund organizations already doing effective research and work in these areas. It hopes that, from the pilot projects it supports, solutions will come that will be effective on a large scale.[4]

Google's responses to these challenge are five initiatives that were chosen out of hundreds of suggestions. Jacquelline Fuller, head of advocacy and communications at Google.org, in commenting on the process of narrowing the philanthropic possibilities down to five initiatives, stated: "There was a lot of tears and angst to go from a white sheet of paper down to five initiatives."[5]

GOOGLE'S FIVE PHILANTHROPIC INITIATIVES

Let's consider the five initiatives that took shape after over a year of research of possible causes to target.

1. Develop Renewable Energy Cheaper than Coal (RE<C)

Google.org is taking on this challenge by forming its own in-house research and development group. It is also supporting research and development through investment and grants to organizations and companies specializing in the renewable energies of solar thermal, wind, and geothermal. Its mission is to replace coal-fired power plants as the cheapest option with a renewable energy. Google.org also intends to promote public policies that speed up the development of renewable energy.

Using the sun to generate power has been around since the oil crisis of the late 1970s and early 1980s. The development of solar power waned after that crisis without government backing and funding for large plants. But now with rising oil prices and growing concern over climate changes, proposed and existing U.S. federal legislation, as well as state laws related to renewable energy already in place in some states, this renewable energy is again attracting investment dollars. The states of Nevada, Arizona, New Mexico, and Colorado now require that between 15 and 20% of their power to come from solar sources. This growing commitment of federal and state governments to renewable energy encourages more research and development.

The Renewable Energy and Energy Conservation Tax Act of 2008, H.R. 5351

The House of Representatives passed the Renewable Energy and Energy Conservation Tax Act of 2008, H.R. 5351, on February 27, 2008. The bill went to the Senate the next day and, after being read twice, was referred to the Senate Committee on Finance. These are the key features of the bill:

- It will end unnecessary subsidies to large oil companies. This subsidy money will instead be used to finance incentives to encourage the development and use of clean renewable energy.
- It will extend and expand tax incentives for plug-in hybrid cars, energy efficient homes, buildings, and appliances.
- It includes over $8 billion in long-term tax incentives for electricity produced from renewable resources, including wind, solar, geothermal, hydropower, ocean tides, biomass, and landfill gas.
- It will provide for $2 billion in bonds for electric co-ops and public power companies to finance clean renewable energy from the renewable resources in the previous point.

House of Representatives Speaker Nancy Pelosi notes on her Web site that the bill will create tens of thousands of jobs and planned renewable energy projects that could provide electricity for up to 12 million homes.

She also puts the benefits of the bill in perspective in terms of what it will mean to the average U.S. citizen when she comments that: "The big five oil companies recently reported record profits for 2007, with ExxonMobil earning $40.6 billion—the largest corporate profit in American history. While oil company profits have quadrupled, high energy prices continue to squeeze American families."[6]

While we can't know at this moment whether the bill will pass—and, if it does, in what exact form—it still represents acknowledgement of the problem of America's reliance on oil and the critical need to find alternative clean and renewable energy sources.

Solar companies are moving into position to compete with natural gas and coal as both become more expensive. Some banks are including the risks of climate change legislation into the costs of their loans for conventional power plants, while solar companies like eSolar are finding ways to reduce the cost of production of the components for their power plants and simplifying construction.[7]

Google has invested $10 million in eSolar, whose core technology is an implementation of concentrating solar power, sometimes referred to as solar thermal. A field of heliostats—instruments that use mirrors to reflect solar heat—direct the heat to a thermal receiver. This concentrated heat boils water in the thermal receiver. The steam that is produced is piped to a turbine that generates power. Cooling converts the steam back to water and the cycle is repeated.[8]

According to eSolar's April 2008 press release, it "has secured land rights in the southwest United States to support the production and transmission of over 1 GW of power. eSolar will have a fully operational power plant later this year in southern California." Google's investment, in combination with funding from Idealab, Oak Investment Partners, and others, brings eSolar's recent funding up to a total of $130 million. Bill Gross, who founded Idealab and Overture, the first search company to match search with relevant advertising, is chairman of eSolar.[9]

Google.org is also investing in the privately held solar company Bright Source. Other investors include BP Alternative Energy and Chevron Technology Ventures. Arthur Goldman, founder and chairman of BrightSource, with a previous company, Luz International Ltd. (no longer in operation), was the first to demonstrate that solar power can be affordably produced in large quantities using solar power. Between 1984 and 1990, Luz built nine solar electricity generating stations in California's Mojave Desert. These plants still operate profitably.[10]

Another Google.org $10 million investment was made in Makani Power to support its research and development on high-altitude wind energy extraction.[11]

Google is demonstrating its commitment to renewable energy in its own operations in several ways. It has installed solar panels at the

Googleplex that generate 1.6 megawatts, which is 30% of the peak power necessary to fuel the buildings on which they are located. They are a good investment and will pay for themselves in seven years. Google intends to install solar modules in its office in Hyderabad, India, that will supply hot water for the building. Google's new facility in Oregon will use cheaper electricity from a nearby hydroelectric plant.

Google's server farms are immense buildings that require a lot of electricity. Tens of thousands of computers running at the same time not only pull a lot of juice, but they need air conditioning to keep them from melting in the heat they generate. For every dollar any company spends to power a typical server, it spends another dollar on air conditioning to keep it cool. So, given that it has at least a half million servers with plans to build more data centers to house more servers, Google has a strong business interest in renewable energy. Not only would employees be better citizens of the planet if they could develop and use renewable energy, the company could also significantly reduce its operating costs.

Richard Wray of *Guardian Unlimited* interviewed Sergey in November 2007 about Google's mixed motives for its initiative to develop renewable energy cheaper than coal. If Google was successful in finding a source of renewable energy cheaper than coal, Wray asked, did the company plan to share that source or would it use it to make a fortune. Sergey responded, "A lot of our approach will focus on partnership and investment and in those cases it is somewhat up to those companies to figure out how to broadly deploy their technology. But to the extent that we have a say in it, we want it to be deployed as widely as possible. We also want that company or division to really benefit and continue to invest in development."[12]

Google is taking seriously its corporate social responsibility to reduce and, hopefully, eventually eliminate the damage to the planet from its own value chain activities. It acknowledges and assumes responsibility for the fact that Google's immense computer infrastructure consumes vast quantities of electricity and therefore contributes to the production of greenhouse gases.

Google made and met a commitment to being carbon-neutral for the year 2007. It pledges to remain so in the future. It is accomplishing this by making its own operations more energy efficient. It is also aggressively researching and investing in alternative energy sources that are clean, renewable, and cheap. The investments in projects that help offset carbon generated are intended to balance the emissions that it can't reduce by direct means yet. For example, Google funded improved animal waste management systems in Mexico and Brazil. Before the funding, the waste runoff from these livestock operations emitted greenhouse gases that were not only deadly to the planet but were locally harming the air quality and contaminating land and water in the local areas in which they operated. While Google recognizes that carbon offsets aren't enough to fundamentally reduce greenhouse emissions over time, the projects it funds result in measurable reductions. These offset projects in combination with other long-term initiatives help Google to take responsibility for its carbon footprint.

Google takes pride in the fact that its data centers use half as much energy as comparable data centers in its industry. It has achieved this by using efficient power supplies and evaporative cooling technology. Furthermore, it is making the lighting in its worldwide offices more energy efficient and performs energy audits to look for additional ways to reduce its use of energy. Google started a Climate Savers Computing Initiative to join with others in the industry to share information about reducing electricity usage.[13]

2. Accelerate the Commercialization of Plug-In Vehicles (RechargeIT)

The goal of the RechargeIT initiative is to reduce CO_2 emissions and oil use through mass commercialization of plug-in vehicles. Google's own fleet of cars is used to demonstrate the plug-in technology.

Google.org's investments in CalCars and its grant to Plug-In America were mentioned at the beginning of the chapter as examples of Google. org's hybrid philanthropic model that takes advantage of the dual strategies of investment and grants to accomplish its goals. In addition to the Plug-In America grant to support advocacy of plug-ins, grants have also been awarded to the Brookings Institution, the Electric Power Research Institute, the Rocky Mountain Institute, and Dr. Willett Kempton at the University of Delaware.

Google.org hosted a conference at the Brookings Institution in June 2008, in Washington, DC, called "Plug-In Electric Vehicles 2008: What Role for Washington?" The conference concentrated on plug-in electric vehicles, analyzing their potential, their feasibility, and the advantages and disadvantages of a variety of federal policies to promote them.[14] Panelists included prominent politicians, industry executives, government regulators, nonprofit executives, and respected journalists served as moderators. One significant event at this conference was the United States Department of Energy (DOE) Assistant Secretary of Energy Efficiency and Renewable Energy Andy Karsner's announcement that up to $30 million in funding over three years for three cost-shared Plug-in Hybrid Electric Vehicles (PHEVs) demonstration and development projects was being made available. He stated at the conference that "The projects announced today demonstrate a shared public-private sector commitment to advance clean vehicle technologies and will help reduce our dependence on foreign oil while also confronting the serious challenge of global climate change."[15]

It is both amazing and commendable that Google.org and Brookings could pull together so many key people around the issue of plug-in vehicles which resulted not only in meaningful dialogue but positive action as well.

Hybrid Car Sales
April 2007 to April 2008

U.S. hybrid car sales increased over 41% between April 2007 and April 2008. Sales of the Toyota Prius hybrid electric sedan increased 61% during the same time period and continue to lead the pack. The Toyota Camry hybrid, named hybrid car of the year for 2008 by hybridcar.com, is in second place.[16]

---

3. Predict and Prevent

Google.org's effort to try to identify infectious diseases before an outbreak is somewhat unusual. Google plans to apply its expertise to disseminate knowledge and to support the collection, sharing, and analysis of data to map the places in the world that are particularly vulnerable to infectious diseases and to "contribute to enhanced resilience of communities to withstand threats and adapt to changes." Google's position is that it can help prevent "localized health crises from becoming regional or global threats by providing timely, accurate, and accessible information."[17]

One of Google.org's first projects born from this vision was to start a new nonprofit organization called Innovative Support to Emergencies, Diseases and Disasters, or Instedd. Instedd will collaborate with scientists, software engineers, health and relief organizations, and governments to develop software and other technologies to enhance sharing of information and teamwork to detect potential hot spots and plan humanitarian responses. Working with 20 partners, Instedd's first project is to identify emerging infectious diseases and improve the ability to respond to them in Cambodia, Laos, Myanmar, Thailand, Vietnam, and Yunnan Province in southern China.

Instedd's software engineers are researching how existing technologies can be repurposed to track diseases and plan responses. They've already succeeded in generating several tools using existing technologies from Microsoft, Google, and Facebook. One of those new tools helps to solve the challenge of quickly translating vital information from one language to another; it is a text-messaging system that allows messages to be written in Khmer, Cambodia's official language, and received in Burmese.

Dr. Eric Rasmussen, chief executive officer for Instedd, explains how early detection of infectious diseases is critical not only to the regions where they immediately appear but to the entire planet: "We are so connected as a global population now with travel and trade. If we do not spot [health] events transpiring early enough, it doesn't take much for them to escape."[18]

Google.org contributed a $5 million grant to Instedd. The new organization also attracted a $1 million grant from the Rockefeller Foundation.

4. Inform and Empower to Improve Public Services

Google.org acknowledges that improving public services and accountability for the quality of the basics of life such as water, sanitation, health services, and education won't be quick in the developing world. But it believes that if it provides communities and policymakers in East Africa and India with relevant and accurate information, it will be a step toward empowering communities in those countries to improve public services. This, in turn, will improve the health of communities and help combat poverty. Communities will receive information about their rights and entitlements relative to the quality of the public services they receive. Google will experiment with different methods and media such as mobile and e-kiosks to deliver information.

At the same time that it is attempting to empower the citizens with information, Google.org will provide policymakers with more information and better information to cope with increased demands for service and problems inherent in delivering those services. Google.org states that:

> To "unlock" existing data that is not publicly available, we are seeking innovations in the way data can be accessed, entered, stored, analyzed and communicated. Google.org believes that the transparency that comes with more public information increases checks and balances between citizens and communities, and policymakers.

Google.org realizes that strong local leadership is critical for success. It also realizes that success may only come if the work spans generations. Google.org is apparently ready for a long-term effort when it states: "We are committed to investing in the next generation of business, government, and civil society leaders to ensure the sustainability of this initiative."[19]

Google.org is also working to improve the flow of information to government officials and lobbying them for change. Charles Moore, the executive director of Paul Newman's Committee Encouraging Corporate Philanthropy (CECP) commented on this approach: "You won't see many companies stepping up and dealing with governments like that."[20]

Google.org is supporting indigenous reform efforts in India, which suggests empowering the communities it wishes to serve rather than just assuming answers from outsiders are better. It awarded $765,000 to the Centre for Budget and Policy Studies, a Bangalore-based analysis group, to create a Budget Information Service for local governments to facilitate better district- and municipal-level planning in India. It gave $660,000 to the Center for Policy Research in India, which is intended to encourage research and debate concerning issues of urban local governance and urban service delivery.

Of particular significance, because of its impact on the entire country, is a $2 million grant to a nonprofit organization in India called Pratham that is committed to improving education. This grant will pay for an independent institute to carry out large-scale assessments of educational programs, including India's Nationwide Annual Status of Education Report (ASER). In the future, the goal will be to conduct assessments of other public service areas.

Dr. Madhav Chava, Pratham's founder and director of programs, commented on the value of Google's grant: "With Google's help we are planning to strengthen ASER in many ways while retaining its voluntary spirit and movement-like character. This partnership will help in creating a new network of people and institutions who will learn better skills of surveying, assessing, and analyzing data."[21]

Improving the quality of education in India is essential to breaking cycles of illiteracy, poverty, and disease from generation to generation. Currently, of the 140 million children in primary schools in India, 30 million cannot read at all, 40 million can identify only a few alphabets, 40 million can read some words, and 30 million can read paragraphs. More than 55 million of these students will drop out of school before completing four years.[22]

The result of a 2007 survey conducted by the Federation of Indian Chambers of Commerce revealed serious shortages in skilled workers, including refrigeration mechanics, electricians, doctors, nurses, and paramedics. Within a few years, the textile and automotive industries are anticipating rapid growth that will require millions of new workers. Meeting these needs will depend on improving the quality of education in the country.[23]

Google's philanthropic focus on India makes sense because the company already has a strong presence in India, and it wants to increase advertising sales there as well. An educated and employed population presents a better market of buyers of products and thus encourages the sale of advertising.

In addition to having several offices in India, Google's first research and development center outside the United States was established in Bangalore in 2004. The reason for choosing Bangalore, according to Sukhinder Singh Cassidy, who is the head of Google's Asia operation, was partly "because so many Googlers who are Indian want to move back to India and participate in India's growth."[24]

Google is extremely popular in India, with an estimated 75% of India's 25 million regular Internet users choosing it as their number one search destination. Google's strategy for generating new advertising markets includes India. While India's current online advertising is only $53 million compared to $16.8 billion spent in the United States, it is expected to grow to almost $600 million by 2009.

India is part of Google's plan to reach the 5.5 billion people on the planet who are not yet on the Internet. Eight times more people in India have mobile phones than have Internet access. Google's development of wireless products indicates that it plans to better serve the Indian market and, in turn, go after a lion's share of the projected advertising dollars that will be spent on online advertising in the near future.

5. Fuel the Growth of Small and Medium-Sized Enterprises

Focusing again on India and East Africa, Google.org intends to promote equitable economic growth by providing support to small and medium-sized enterprises (SMEs). Small and medium-sized businesses are underfinanced in many developing countries compared to larger and micro-entrepreneurs, both of which are well supported by banks. Google.org believes that, by making expertise and capital available to SMEs, it will support the growth of these businesses and the creation of more jobs. This, in turn, strengthens the whole economies of these countries.

GOOGLE.ORG'S GRANT ACTIVITY

Google.org's commitment to addressing the problem of climate change led to a $617,457 grant to Clark University in Worcester, Massachusetts, for a project exploring whether there are patterns that could be isolated and used to forecast droughts before they begin. The project involves the analysis of 50 years of data on Africa's climate, deforestation, and soil moisture. The Gordon and Betty Moore Foundation in San Francisco has contributed an equal amount to support the project.

Google.org has awarded grants totaling $4.7 million to TechnoServe. Since 2006, Google.org has granted TechnoServe $1.7 million to manage business plan competitions and entrepreneurship programs in Tanzania and Ghana. A $3.7 million general support grant was awarded to TechnoServe's project to support businesses and antipoverty programs and to create jobs in Africa. The Grameen Foundation received $200,000 to research the potential of mobile applications to provide information to households and rural enterprise initiatives in East Africa.

A $5.2 million award to the Acumen Fund helps build businesses that provide services to the poor using market-based approaches. A $2.5 million grant was awarded to the Global Health and Security Initiative to track international biological threats. These are just a representative sample of Google.org's large grants.

Special projects and learning grants include $50,000 for climate change research to the Energy Foundation; $100,000 to support the implementation of the Global Warming Solutions Act of 2006; and $2 million toward the establishment of a Center on Energy Efficiency Standards that, through mandatory and voluntary efficiency standards for appliances, equipment, and buildings, help the United States and China reduce global warming pollution. Google.org has also contributed over $3 million to disaster relief and recovery in the wake of Hurricane Katrina, the central China earthquake, and Cyclone Nagris in Myanmar.

GOOGLE.ORG'S STAFF

Google spent a over a year doing research before it launched Google.org. It currently has a staff of 40 with widely diverse backgrounds. A former assistant secretary of energy for the U.S. government, a former vice president at Goldman Sachs, and an epidemiologist are just a few members of the team of experts at Google.org.

Larry Brilliant is the first executive director of Google.org. Around the time of his appointment in February 2006, Brilliant said: "In 10 years, I'd like people to say Google changed the world less for its search engine than for the way in which it changed philanthropy to make the world a better place."[25]

Brilliant has amazing credentials to bring to Google's philanthropic effort. He's a physician; epidemiologist; former associate professor of epidemiology, global health planning, and economic development at the University of Michigan; and former CEO of technology companies. After receiving his medical degree, Brilliant studied for two years with a Hindu guru in India. His guru, Neem Karoli Baba, shortly before his death, told Brilliant to leave the ashram and use his medical knowledge and skills to combat smallpox, which was taking a heavy toll in India during the early 1970s. Brilliant managed 100,000 workers who eliminated smallpox in India over a two-year period after he joined the World Health Organization as a medical officer. He returned to the United States and started the Society for Epidemiology and Voluntary Assistance—a foundation that has performed more than two million operations and is credited with restoring more sight than any other organization in the world.[26]

Dr. Brilliant was working in India with the United Nations program to eradicate polio when he first read about Google.org in a local paper. But he didn't even receive a response to the email he sent to info@google.com.

In 2006, he was awarded the TED Prize at the Annual Technology, Entertainment and Design Conference, which consisted of $100,000 and a "wish" for how to change the world. Brilliant's wish was for a system that would detect early and rapidly respond to outbreaks of disease. He envisioned an open-source public access network to help his wish come true. Some Googlers invited Brilliant to speak at the company after hearing about the award. After hearing his talk, Larry Page and Eric Schmidt knew they had found their first director for Google.org.

THE FUTURE OF GOOGLE.ORG

Google.org's approach to philanthropy has gathered compliments from within the world of corporate giving. Charles Moore, the executive director of Paul Newman's Committee Encouraging Corporate Philanthropy commented, "I respect companies' innovation in addressing how they invest in their communities in all ways. I think what they're doing is quite extraordinary and unique."[27]

Committee Encouraging Corporate Philanthropy

Paul Newman, actor, director, entrepreneur, and philanthropist, along with former Goldman Sachs cochairman John C. Whitehead and New York real estate investor and lawyer Peter Malkin, started the Committee Encouraging Corporate Philanthropy in November 1999. CECP is "the only international forum of business CEOs and Chairpersons pursuing a mission focused exclusively on corporate philanthropy."[28]

CECP's mission is to provide leadership, advocacy, education and research to corporations to encourage corporate philanthropy and to improve its quality. Its membership is by invitation only, and membership is reviewed annually. It currently includes more than 165 CEOs and chairpersons, some of whom are leaders of the largest companies in the world, such as American Express, Bank of America, Mitsubishi International, General Mills, Time Warner, IBM, General Electric, Chevron, The Coca Cola Company, Xerox, Nokia, and the Blackstone Group, to name a few.

In 2002, CECP created an online survey and reporting tool called the Corporate Giving Standard. More than 136 companies participate in the survey. The report generated by the survey serves as a benchmarking tool for members. The report also features case studies and tips and tools for using the data in the report.

Paul Newman captures the spirit of the organization and his feelings about it when he states: "I helped to start CECP with the belief that corporate America could be a force for good in society. I'm immensely proud of and inspired by all CECP members, who have risen to this challenge and accepted their responsibility to the global community."[29]

Yet others who watch and analyze corporate philanthropic efforts wonder whether Google has taken on challenges that are too complex for any corporation, even though it is developing a remarkable collaborative model working with citizens, governments, existing nonprofits, and financial institutions in the countries it hopes to serve. Some market analysts question how Google's foray into renewable energy research might change the landscape of the energy industry given that its success would make it a rival to companies who produce coal and oil. Will there be a backlash from companies who buy advertising from Google? These questions will be answered over time. Meanwhile, Google's philanthropic efforts remain one more facet of the company to watch that seems to thrive on doing things its own way and trying to change the world for better through application of its core competencies.[30]

NOTES

1. http://www.google.com/support/jobs/bin/topic.py?loc_id=1116&dep_id=10093 (accessed April 15, 2008).

2. http://www.google.org/foundation.html (accessed May 20, 2008).

3. http://www.google.org/about.html (accessed May 18, 2008).

4. Larry Brilliant, "New Team Members for Google.org," The Official Google Blog, April 6, 2007, http://googleblog.blogspot.com/2007/04/new-team-members-for-googleorg.html (accessed April 8, 2008).

5. Nicole Wallace, "Climate Change and Poverty Top Google's Giving Priorities," *Chronicle of Philanthropy,* January 17, 2008, http://www.philanthropy.com/news/updates/index.php?id=3783 (accessed April 19, 2008).

6. http://www.speaker.gov/legislation?id=0162 (accessed May 24, 2008).

7. Alexis Madrigal, "Google-Backed Solar Startup Picks up Steam, $130 Million," *Wired,* April 21, 2008, http://www.wired.com/science/planetearth/news/2008/04/solar_thermal (accessed May 23, 2008); Jennifer Kho, "Ausra Raises $40M for Concentrating Solar-Thermal," Greentech Media, September 11, 2007, http://www.greentechmedia.com/articles/ausra-raises-40m-for-concentrating-solar-thermal.html (accessed May 23, 2008).

8. http://www.esolar.com/solution.html (accessed May 24, 2008).

9. "eSolar Announces Breakthrough Pre-Fabricated Solar Power Plants," eSolar, April 21, 2008, http://www.esolar.com/news/press/2008_04_21 (accessed May 23, 2008).

10. http://www.brightsourceenergy.com/about.htm (accessed May 24, 2008).

11. "Grants and Investments," http://www.google.org/projects.html (accessed May 26, 2008).

12. Richard Wray, "Google To Invest Millions in Green Energy," *The Guardian,* November 28, 2007, http://www.guardian.co.uk/business/2007/nov/28/google.greenbusiness (accessed April 21, 2008).

13. "Powering a Clean Energy Revolution," http://www.google.com/corporate/green/energy/reducing.html (accessed April 9, 2008).

14. "Plug-In Electric Vehicles 2008: What Role for Washington?" Brookings Events, http://www.brookings.edu/events/2008/0611_plugin_vehicle.aspx (assessed June 28, 2008).

15. "DOE Announces $30 Million for Plug-in Hybrid Electric Vehicle Projects," U.S. Department of Energy, June 12, 2008, http://www.doe.gov/news/6337.htm (accessed June 29, 2008).

16. http://www.hybridcar.com/index.php?option=com_content&task=view&id=612&Itemid=45 (accessed May 26, 2008).

17. "Predict and Prevent," http://www.google.org/predict.html (accessed April 4, 2008).

18. Nicole Wallace, "Climate Change and Poverty Top Google's Giving Priorities," *Chronicle of Philanthropy*, January 17, 2008, http://www.philanthropy.com/news/updates/index.php?id=3783 (accessed March 27, 2008).

19. "Inform and Empower to Improve Public Services," http://www.google.org/inform.html (accessed March 25, 2008).

20. Elinor Mills, "Doing Philanthropy the Google Way," CNET News.com, January 17, 2008, http://www.news.com/Doing-philanthropy-the-Google-way/2100-1030_3-6226728.html?tag=item (accessed March 28).

21. "Google Awards $2 Million to Pratham for ASER," PrathamUSA, http://www.prathamusa.org/dnn/Google/tabid/100/Default.aspx (accessed April 4, 2008).

22. http://www.pratham.org (accessed April 4, 2008).

23. Andy Mukherjee, "Google, Gates, Indian Diaspora Bet on Children," *Bloomberg.com*, February 26, 2008, http://www.bloomberg.com/apps/news?pid=20601039&sid=apnpCWrLAUsc&refer=home (accessed April 13, 2008).

24. Sheridan Prasso, "Google Goes to India," *Fortune*, October 23, 2007, http://money.cnn.com/2007/10/18/news/international/google_india.fortune/index.htm (accessed April 13, 2008).

25. Jessi Hempel, "Google's Brilliant Philanthropist," *BusinessWeek*, February 22, 2006, http://www.businessweek.com/technology/content/feb2006/tc20060222_088020.htm (accessed April 7, 2008).

26. Katie Hafner, "Philanthropy Google's Way: Not the Usual," *New York Times*, September 14, 2006, http://www.nytimes.com/2006/09/14/technology/14google.html?pagewanted=all (accessed April 19, 2008).

27. Elinor Mills, "Doing Philanthropy The Google Way," *NET News.com* January 17, 2008, http://news.cnet.com/Doing-philanthropy-the-Google-way/2100-1030_3-6226728.html (accessed April 10, 2008).

28. http://www.corporatephilanthropy.org/overview (accessed May 1, 2008).

29. Ibid.

30. Kevin J. Delaney, "Google: From 'Don't Be Evil' to How to Do Good," *Wall Street Journal*, January 18, 2008, http://www.idealab.com/frame.php?referer=/press_room/&url=http%3A//online.wsj.com/article/SB120058125428197687.html%3Fmod%3Dgooglenews_wsj (accessed April 29, 2008).

Chapter Eight

Google and Education

Google's commitment to education is a natural extension of its mission "to organize the world's information and make it universally accessible and useful."[1] Google has the potential to educate any individuals who use it to search Web-based documents; its collection of digitized books, video, and images; and Google news, to name just a few. And, while users are being informed and educated by search results, Google is generating revenue through discrete ads relevant to the information that was sought.

Advertisers who sell products aimed at educators and students will want to spend their online advertising dollars where there is the most online traffic for their products. More generally, advertisers with products to sell young people will also seek high-traffic sites. There are more than 43 million children in school in the United States. Elementary school children have approximately $15 billion per year in their own spending money, and they influence $160 billion of spending money that their parents control. Teenagers spend $57 billion of their own money per year and $36 billion that is part of their parents' income.[2]

Google generated 99% of its revenue for the years 2005 to 2007 from its advertisers. With almost all of its revenue dependent on attracting as many users as possible to maintain its appeal to advertisers, Google is compelled to attract audiences by not just offering pure search, but by offering free services and products to attract customers.

HOW GOOGLE REACHES EDUCATORS

Google aggressively reaches out to K–12 educators on its Web site to inform them of what it has to offer. In this way, it not only attracts dollars for advertisers from educators using Google search and Google tools, but it reaches young people as well who use Google search in their classrooms as well as at home.

Google provides the means for two-way communication with educators on its Web site through the Google for Educators Discussion Group (groups.google.com/group/google-for-educators), which gives teachers a way to exchange and share ideas as well as a way for Google to update the education community about its new offerings for K–12 educators. Google also extends an invitation to educators to submit examples of how they use Google in their classrooms while also offering a page where teachers can peruse examples that have already been submitted by teachers and librarians.

Google sponsors the Google Teacher Academy, which gives teachers the chance to become certified in using Google tools. Currently, there are 150 Google certified teachers nationwide. Google certified teachers are described as having "a passion for using innovative tools to improve teaching and learning" who "can spread innovation as a recognized expert." At the end of the Academy, they are expected to complete a personal action plan to define how they will "extend their learning to their community."[3]

AN INTERVIEW WITH AN EDUCATION EXPERT

To get an expert's view of how Google tools are used in the classroom and to what extent they are used, I interviewed educational consultant Chris O'Neal by e-mail and by phone to get some answers to questions as well as an insider's perspective. Chris received teacher of the year honors during his time as an elementary and middle school teacher in Louisiana. He also chaired the mayor's Committee for Youth Leadership for the city of Lake Charles. He left the classroom to work in his school's district office, where he provided professional development to teachers and administrators, especially in high-risk schools. He then worked at the Louisiana State Department of Education, eventually becoming the state director of technology.

Chris now teaches at the University of Virginia and works with the Virginia Department of Education to provide outreach and professional development to school administrators. Chris also is a featured speaker each year at the National Educational Computing Conference and serves as a faculty associate for the George Lucas Educational Foundation.[4]

Because of his observations of technology use in Virginia classrooms and other states as an educational consultant and his active involvement with national and international professional organizations concerned with technology and education, Chris is well qualified to share his insights about how Google tools are used by educators.

VS: Chris, what's your overall impression of how educators and students have reacted to Google's Tools for Educators?

CO: Google's array of free tools has reached huge international popularity amongst students and teachers in both the primary and secondary level. Educators across the world have embraced the suite of utilities that Google has developed the last few years, and students have learned that they can use most of these tools both in and out of the classroom for free. More and more classrooms are finding that these Web 2.0 tools offer great flexibility and since the work that's done with them is online, teachers and students can work on them anywhere they have access to the Web.

What Is Web 2.0?

Sounds like a software application, doesn't it? But it's not. Web 2.0 refers to all the Web-based tools that allow for audience participation, networking, and getting information out with ease. A great example would be wikis; a great example of a wiki is Wikipedia. In the early days of the Web, you'd go to a site to read entries from the *Encyclopedia Britannica*. That would be Web 1.0. Today, you go to Wikipedia and not only read about something but add to the knowledge bank yourself by adding your own take on a subject or disputing the ideas of someone else. That's Web 2.0.

Blogging is another great example of Web 2.0. Instead of a static Web site where the pages basically stay the same except for periodic updates (Web 1.0), blogging can be fresh daily, provide a means for just about anybody to get content on the Web, and, if they want, provide feedback to bloggers or dialogue with other readers. That's Web 2.0.

Gone are the days when you had to check your favorite news site or blog to see what's new (Web 1.0). Now you can sign up for RSS feeds and have all that delivered right to your e-mail box (Web 2.0).

YouTube, social bookmarking, audio and video streaming, podcasts—the list of Web 2.0 tools is huge and growing, and the best part is that all of these services are free. If rich user experience, user participation, and dynamic content are the primary characteristics of Web 2.0 tools, then which Google tools do you think would be considered Web 2.0 tools?

VS: I notice that to help educators understand how to use Google in the classroom, Google has organized its free tools on its Web page for educators into three categories: search; communicate, show, and share; and newly featured products (www.google.com/edu cators/tools.html). It also offers educational institutions a Google Apps Education Edition for purchase that includes Google technical support.

What's more, in the tools for educators in the search category, Google includes Book Search, Earth, Maps, News, iGoogle, and Web Search. Would you share your insights about some of these tools?

CO: Google Maps is one of Google's most ubiquitous tools. It's been around for years, and has helped many users find their way around, plan trips, and calculate driving directions. Mapping and geography skills are, of course, huge learning objectives in the education environment. Teachers are finding very involved uses for Google Maps in every grade level.

Younger learners can learn about distance, time, and basic map topography. Teachers zoom in on locations, then zoom out to help primary students grasp the concept of locations within locations, and to understand the relationship between city, state, country, and so on. They can also begin to understand map scale as the teacher demonstrates moving from point A to point B. The students can get "hands on" with a map and gain hugely valuable insight as they draw maps from school to home, for example. With overlay features of terrain, satellite and, in some cases even traffic, the possibilities are endless as far as learning opportunities in the classroom.

Teachers have learned to make interdisciplinary units with the maps tool by merging it with other Google tools such as Google Docs. Students can plan their ultimate road trip, while keeping a journal of it in Google Docs, mapping out the path in Google Maps and, using Google's landmark points feature, highlight stops along the way. A teacher can make this quite an intense learning experience by providing grading rubrics which specify the use of math skills for gas approximation, or history and research skills in which students must describe landmarks along the way. Students can work collaboratively to decide upon meeting points along the way, and use Google spreadsheets to design a budget for the entire trip. The tool is a functional map skill-building tool at the very least, but as teachers learn to integrate it, it becomes a solid thread throughout some very well done units.

VS: I'm curious about whether iGoogle is used in the schools. I know that controlling which sites children can visit is a big issue in school. Will you explain how iGoogle works and whether it addresses security issues?

CO: iGoogle helps teachers in relation to security and some other significant issues, but I'll explain what it is first before I get into that. iGoogle is an RSS aggregator home page, designed to put all your blog subscriptions, newsfeeds, podcasts, and other information sources in one easy to view place. Using the iGoogle homepage, users can easily merge their various RSS-based subscriptions into a clean interface, making it incredibly efficient and simple to keep track of hundreds of information sources. One issue that teachers often have with technology in the classroom is that the time it takes to use the tool simply cannot outweigh its benefit. Blogs, wikis, and other information sources are fantastic in the classroom, but if too much time is spent just getting to those sources, and not enough time analyzing and using the information itself, it simply isn't a practical approach in the busy day of a school.

iGoogle solves that problem quite easily in that a teacher can decide ahead of time which blogs are safe, most relevant, and timely for his or her classroom needs. Those information sources can be dropped into an iGoogle page, making one "home base" from which students can view the various information sources, explore, research, and so on.

This personalized home page is built on "gadgets." A gadget, in this case, is simply a customizable module that fits on the page. An iGoogle single page might contain a dozen gadgets ranging from a handful of content-related blogs, to some targeted sections of an online encyclopedia, to selected weather modules. Perhaps a teacher is studying climate across the world. She could set up an iGoogle page with one module per country of study, such that each module displayed the current weather and climate related information.

Many teachers are using iGoogle as their default homepage for their browsers at school. This allows students to immediately start at a base of information specifically geared toward current lessons. At any point, the teacher can change the modules while Google's RSS feeds refresh the content. It's a nice way to take advantage of a wealth of information sources but in a streamlined, time-saving way.

VS: The second category of Google tools are designated as tools to "communicate, share, and show" on their Web site. They include Blogger, Calendar, Docs, Groups, Page Creator, Picasa, and SketchUp. What's your take on the value of some of the tools in this category for classroom use?

CO: Electronic calendars certainly aren't new to the technology world. But, integration and synchronization are only recently making it to the top of the calendar feature list. Organizations of all kinds have used electronic calendars as a way to keep workers in the loop with important meetings, project deadlines, and the like. Project management has become a core function for employees at all levels. Therefore, the need to manage a calendar, synchronize with others, and keep tabs on time, dates, and deadlines is a powerful set of skills that every high school graduate should bring to the workforce.

In addition to Gmail and Google Docs, Google's calendar tool has become a solid piece of Google's tools that schools are making use of across the world. The calendar tool allows a schoolwide calendar to be kept online and easily updated in a collaborative fashion much like Google Docs. It helps to keep everyone aware of meetings, school functions, testing and examination dates, holidays, and so on. Further, if the calendar is made shareable to parents via the Web, it helps prevent once again parents missing out on key events due to their child losing the traditional paper calendar. Since these calendars are published via RSS feed, parents and the educational community can subscribe to a calendar and always be notified of important events.

One handy feature of Google calendars is the option to send a text message or e-mail reminder about specific calendar occurrences. As more and more teachers are finding out about this tool, they are realizing it's not only a huge time saver, but a huge paper saver as well. Calendars don't have to be reprinted when there's a change, a teacher can have master calendars with schoolwide dates, and then individual calendars specific to each period they teach. They can manage these calendars from any computer, and "push out" information, additional reminders, and resources attached to specific dates.

VS: Are there any other tools in this category that you see being used in the classroom?

CO: Google's Sketchup tool is a downloadable application that is slowly making its way into classrooms. Students love to create and design. It's human nature, fun, and is the cornerstone to education. Sketchup is 3-D modeling software that allows students to create virtual buildings, homes, and playgrounds. It is literally a blank canvas where students can use a myriad of geometry skills to create their own ultimate bedroom, for example. Elementary students who are just learning the concepts of shape, scale, area, and perimeter can play with "living" shapes that take on different capacities, measurements, colors, textures, etc. Older students could be given parameters by which to design their first home. So a teacher might allow each student so many square feet to work with. Given that, students would employ literally dozens of measuring, estimating, and design skills as they work on something real-world and completely engrossing. Teachers often struggle to connect mathematical concepts to real world, and keep the students' interest. This is one of the rare tools that does just that. Teachers can demonstrate for a group of students the core concepts of area, perimeter, measurement, and so on, then students can take the lead as they build 3-D models. The tool provides yet another chance for classrooms to engage in collaborative learning as groups of students could work together to build an amusement park, or a fantasy island, or a sports arena—all of which could contain research, mathematical competencies, and countless collaboration and cooperation skills.

VS: Speaking of collaborative learning, what do you think about Google Docs? Many academics and business people I've talked to use it for projects that require collaboration.

CO: Google Docs offers the option for real-time online collaboration. The basic office suite package provides word processing, spreadsheets, and presentations all built within one Web-based package. Each of these tools works in conjunction with the other to provide an integrated suite that offers real-time online collaboration.

Teachers can work together using one Google word processing document, for example, to collaboratively write a grant. In the past, just as in the business world, one of the writers might make a draft and send it on to their peers to review and add additional information. Once that author finished with her editing, she would forward a revised copy back to the team. This process could produce numerous versions with numerous edits with countless revisions by the time the final version was decided upon. Writing within a collaborative tool like Google Docs alleviates this problem because there is technically only one document, living online. Each author is simply contributing to a single, jointly written document with no fears of editing the wrong version or losing track of one contributor's input. A "doc" in Google Docs keeps a history of every saved revision, so users can watch the progress unfold, compare revisions, and never worry that they may overwrite a good version accidentally.

Take this notion into the classroom for student-collaborative writing, and you can see why teachers are using these tools more and more. Traditionally, a group-authored project in the classroom might mean that one student does the writing while the others watch. Further, the teacher had little ability to truly see who had contributed what, and to what degree legitimate collaboration took place. Using Google Docs in the classroom might take this scenario: A teacher assigns a group of students to research and write a political statement from a certain time in history. The teacher creates a Google Doc blank starting page online. Each student logs in from their Google account, and must contribute equally, which would entail original writing, reviewing other student work, offering suggestions, and working together to eventually revise this work into a final product. Since the document tracks each author's work separately, the teacher can see exactly how the collaborative process unfolds. Since students only need a Web browser to use this document tool, they can log in from any computer, regardless of whether it has an office suite installed. Perhaps most importantly, since the document lives online, there is no chance for the old "I forgot my work at home."

Google Docs offers security as well, such that only allowed users can see the document and make contributions. At any point, a teacher could stop the writing process, or remove a writer, or even add additional teammates to the pool. Since the documents are all housed online, each person can contribute from anywhere with Internet access. Finally, Google Docs offers the ability to publish as well. So, once a document has reached the final stage, students can publish their work to the world with a single click.

VS: What about the spreadsheets and the presentation tool?

CO: The spreadsheets and presentation tool work in the same manner. The documents that are created are stored and saved online. Each document can be created privately, and simply edited in much the same way a user would edit any other spreadsheet or presentation. But the real power of this suite comes in the collaboration capabilities. Students could all work together on data collection, and have one single document in which to store the data. The presentation tool is the perfect opportunity for students to learn to create, edit, and prepare a presentation together. In presentation mode, the Google Docs Presentation tool allows presentation viewers to chat real-time with the presenters, making the entire experience a true group effort. The entire Google Docs suite is quite a well-rounded package for publishing, collaborating, and extending traditional classroom learning assignments beyond the traditional four walls of the classroom.

VS: Are there any other tools in the communicate, show, and share category that you see getting used in classrooms?

CO: Picasa, Google's photo editing, management, and publishing tool is a nice utility to help classrooms manage their digital photos. Teachers have long used digital photography as a way to create classroom portfolios of learning, informal yearbooks, and supplements to lesson plans and units. Picasa is a way to manage all those photos, catalog and tag them, make minor edits, and publish them to a secure area online, or share with the rest of the world. Children love digital photography and, in recent years, classrooms have begun to capitalize on this with the concept of digital storytelling in which students use digital photographs as another layer of expression while they storyboard, write, edit, and publish work with their peers.

Picasa is getting more and more popular with teachers as their folders full of digital images grow, and as the students become more sophisticated in their ability to work with these images. Picasa could be used to simply manage and catalog images, but better yet teachers find it's a fantastic repository so students always have a bank of self-created artwork and photos from which they can pull for presentations, creative writing, and productions, all without having to purchase expensive clip art or commercial photographs. Like most of these other tools, there is also a built in publishing feature which allows students to share their work with rest of the world.

VS: Chris, I'm curious about the extent to which teachers and students statewide and nationwide received training in how to use Google. Since you visit so many schools in Virginia and are in a position to know trends nationwide, what's your sense of efforts to train teachers to use Google?

CO: I'm not aware of specific national or regional professional development or training going on that's Google-specific, other than Google's own educator resources available from http://www.google.com/educators/index.html. Outside that, I use them in numerous workshops around the country with principals and teachers, and I know that many technology coordinators are beginning to introduce Google tools as well, as an alternative to traditional office suites. I'm encouraging educators that I work with to use these tools for a number of reasons. First, they're free and since education typically has budget constraints, that alone is a top reason. Second, and even more importantly, the tools all offer such customization that every teacher across every grade level can make use of the suite of tools.

VS: Are technology standards in schools a factor in how Google is used in the classroom?

CO: In regard to technology standards, ISTE has released a new set of technology standards for students. These standards speak

---

International Society for Training in Education

The International Society for Technology in Education (ISTE) (www.iste.org) is a nonprofit organization with a membership of more than 85,000 education professionals worldwide. It provides leadership in promoting the effective use of technology in PreK–12 schools. ISTE's National Educational Technology Standards is a project that has helped generate standards for student performance related to technology. The standards are now used in all states in the United States and in many other countries. Since 2006, ISTE has started to focus on the next generation of technology standards for students that include creativity, innovation, communication, collaboration, research and information fluency, critical thinking, digital citizenship, and technology operations and concepts.[5]

---

to a much higher level of technology use than standards from years ago. In these standards, students are expected to customize, communicate, collaborate, and publish in numerous ways. What's nice about the Google tools is that they are easy vehicles for educators to address these standards in fun ways.

VS: So, overall, what's your assessment of how well Google is providing tools that are universally appropriate for classroom use?

CO: The tools such as the ones we've talked about in this interview are typically a solid fit in any classroom since most teachers want to be able to customize and tweak software and Internet utilities to meet the needs of various learners. As for students, they have a natural interest in technology, and bring a tech savviness to the table that many teachers themselves don't have.

These tools meet both these needs in that they're easy to use, free or very inexpensive, and very customizable. When modern technology tools make a strong impact in a classroom, it benefits the learning process well beyond the school year—it ensures that students graduating are ready to enter the workforce with technology skills woven into traditional content areas. It also provides a wealth of opportunities for teachers to engage students at higher levels, and make the teacher planning and management side fun as well.

Google has capitalized on the popularity of its tools with educators. There are numerous free online Google groups specifically designed for educators where teachers can talk about lesson planning, appropriate uses of the tools, ways to modify existing tool sets for various classroom uses, and so on. Google has created an online community of educators in this way who dialogue with each other and who provide valuable information to Google as they continue to improve tools and offer new ones.

WHAT DO STUDENTS THINK ABOUT GOOGLE?

I wanted to get a sense of what students thought about Google and how they used it for educational purposes. Although it's impossible to generalize from the responses of just two students, they do provide some food for thought. For those of us over a certain age, we can remember what it was like to go through school without Google and also what a thrill it was to get our own encyclopedia at home. For Jessie and Seth, it's clear they've grown up taking for granted that much of the information about the world is just a click away after they type their query into the Google search box.

Jessie and Seth are the daughter and son of middle-class parents. Both parents are well-educated professionals. The family lives in a small town with a population of slightly over 21,000. Jessie and Seth attend public school. They took time out of their busy teenager lives to give me succinct and interesting answers to a few questions.

VS: What grade are you in?

Seth: Ninth grade.

Jessie: Eleventh grade.

VS: When did you start using Google?

Seth: Around fifth grade when I looked up things for school.

Jessie: In elementary school. It seems like I've always used it.

VS: Did you learn how to use it at school or did you teach yourself?

Seth: I don't remember anyone really teaching me to use it. My sister used it all the time so I guess I learned from watching her.

Jessie: I taught myself.

VS: When do you use Google for school?

Seth: I use it for homework and for projects and reports. I use it for all subjects.

Jessie: All the time for everything.

VS: Can you give me some specific examples of how you use it?

Seth: Whenever I have to create information posters I get information and pictures from Google searches.

Jessie: Spark notes, AP history notes, foreign language translations, current events, Gmail and to get to my usual Web sites that I like to use. I'm sure there are other things that I'm just not thinking of right now.

VS: What features of Google do you use for school?

Seth: I use search, Images, Maps, and Google Earth.

Jessie: Gmail, search, Images; I use the drop-down menu under More to get to other sites.

VS: Do you use Google for fun? If so, how?

Seth: I like using Google Earth.

Jessie: I like to look stuff up for fun: music, questions that I have, Wikipedia. I use Google for everything. It's the only search engine I ever use.

VS: How has Google changed how you learn?

Seth: It provides quick access to information.

Jessie: I have easy access to everything so I feel like I'm better informed. It's easy to get so many references.

VS: What would life without Google be like?

Seth: I'd have to go to the library more.

Jessie: Hell! It would suck not being able to look anything up. It's all at the click of a button.

In a video titled *Inside Google*, Larry Page commented that it was his belief that, because Google made so much of the world's information quickly available, students in the future would not have to commit so much information to memory. If this turns out to be true, then presumably that extra cognitive space and time could be used for creativity and real-world problem solving in schools.

TOOLS FOR LIFELONG LEARNING

Some of Google's education tools attract learners of all ages and those who teach them—from kindergarten to adult learning that extends over a lifetime beyond the years of formal schooling. Google Book Search (www.google.com/educators/p_booksearch.html) is one of those services.

Google Book Search is still in Beta (which means it's still being tested and developed) and is designed to let students of all ages search for digitized books. Some books that are in the public domain and no longer subject to copyright laws are available for free. Those that are still copyrighted can be used for a fee. It is a useful tool for finding out-of-print titles. Google adds value to this service by including extra information such as links to book reviews and online locations where books can be purchased.

Google News (www.google.com/educators/p_news.html) is a valuable resource for any student doing research on current events. Entering a search topic in the Google News search box will yield newspaper and magazine articles from all over the world related to that topic. Archived news going back more than 200 years is also available. The availability of these primary sources for a given time period can help teachers create authentic learning contexts for students who can experience historic events through the words of those who lived during the time in which events took place.

Google Notebook (www.google.com/educators/p_notebook.html) is listed on the page of tools for educators as a new product. It's a research tool for educators and students who wish to add excerpts from text, images, and links from Web pages to their personal online notebook without leaving their browser window. Because it's Web based, the notebook can be accessed from any computer and from a mobile phone. It's possible to create multiple notebooks for different topics, and notebooks can be divided into sections. It's a step up from just bookmarking sites, because users can add notes as they go about sites they might want to revisit in the future. Sharing the notebook is also an option, as is collaboration within a shared notebook.

The Google Custom Search Engine (www.google.com/educators/p_cse.html) is a powerful option for educators. It enables educators to select which Web sites can be searched by students. This is especially valuable for K–12 educators who need to provide sites that are safe for their students. Educators for all students can select sites that are relevant to the topic under study, which saves students' time and focuses their research on the best sources of information.

Educators receive their own URL for their landing page for their custom search engine, and they can customize the look of that landing page. Teachers can collaborate to create a custom search engine that they can use in their individual classrooms, adding more sites to it over time.

Google Scholar (scholar.google.com) is a tool appropriate for high school students, college students, and educators that enables search of scholarly sources. The sources searched include theses, abstracts, articles, and books. Google Scholar returns results after attempting to evaluate material using the same criteria that researchers use, such as the source of the publication, the author, and the extent to which it has been cited in other scholarly work.

A New Google Education Tool on the Horizon

In December 2007, Google invited a group of experts to experiment with its new tool, Knol. Knol stands for a unit of knowledge. Google invited this selected group to write an article on a subject on which they are an authority.

Unlike Wikipedia, which does not publish the names of the authors of entries, Google will publish authors' names with the pieces they write. Google will provide tools for writing and editing of the Knols and also provide free hosting of the content.

Google clearly will be competing with Wikipedia once the tools become available to the public. Google hopes that its Knols will be the first stop for people seeking information on any topic. It anticipates that there will be multiple Knols with different perspectives on many topics.

Readers of Knols will be able to interact with the author by asking questions and adding comments, and they will be able to rate and write reviews of Knols. Knols will include references and links to additional information.

Authors of Knols will have the option to generate income from their writing by opting for Google to match ads to their content. Google will give the authors a share of the revenue from the proceeds of the displayed ads.

This new tool, by the way, is another example of a Web 2.0 application. It seems like it has the potential to offer remedies for some of the shortcomings of the popular Wikipedia—namely, offer the names of authors and their credentials to be writing on a topic.

ONLINE HIGHER EDUCATION

Most U.S. colleges and universities offer online courses to meet the demands of college students who want flexibility to work on their undergraduate and graduate degrees while they work and/or raise families. Because the contact with faculty in online courses relies on primarily asynchronous discussion, Google search is a natural tool for students to enrich discussions quickly and almost effortlessly. I have taught online courses for six years and I continue to be amazed by how easily students move from the discussion forum to Google search to find and share additional information and then return to the online discussion. Because the class discussion is already taking place online, using Google search as a research source becomes part of the discussion flow. And, for students working at home, usually at the end of their work days far from a good library, this is an extremely valuable tool for them.

GOOGLE'S SUCCESS WITH THE EDUCATION MARKET

Google search and its array of tools for educators and students have added value to the educational experience of students of all ages. As mentioned, Google has created on its Web site a community forum for K–12 educators who share how they use Google tools. Google invites them to share and provide feedback on the tools to inform its own research and development.

By making a concerted effort to serve this audience, Google attracts students from an early age who will most likely become lifelong users of Google and potential buyers of products advertised on Google. And there is no reason to doubt that Google's interest in supporting education is genuine. But to keep developing and offering education tools and search, the company must generate income. By increasing the number of customers to its site by attracting students and educators, Google is able to generate the revenue it needs to keep developing new education tools.

NOTES

1. http://www.google.com/corporate (accessed May 1, 2008).

2. "Captive Kids: A Report on Commercial Pressures on Kids at School," Consumers Union, http://www.consumersunion.org/other/captivekids/pressures.htm (accessed April 22, 2008).

3. "Google Certified Teachers," Google for Educators, http://www.google.com/educators/gtc.html (accessed April 23, 2008).

4. Chris O'Neal, "Ed Leaders Online," http://edleadersonline.com/WordPress/?page_id=7 (accessed April 20, 2008).

5. http://www.iste.org/AM/Template.cfm?Section=NETS (accessed April 26, 2008).

Chapter Nine

Using Google to Make Money

In chapter 6, we explored how Google helps us have fun while it attracts traffic to its site to make money. In this chapter, we'll use fictitious scenarios to give you ideas of how to make money using Google and, hopefully, have some fun letting our imaginations run a little wild. We'll also note how Google makes money helping us to make money.

USING GOOGLE TO ESTABLISH A BUSINESS—
THE CORGI'S CUPCAKE

Starting a business is never easy. Although Google can't help with the initial idea or start-up—other than searching the Web to see if anyone's beat us to the punch—it can be vital in helping that new business grow. Michael was taking a break from community college and trying to think of an idea for his own business. He came up with the idea of The Corgi's Cupcake, a gourmet pet bakery that specialized in cupcakes for dogs. But how could he get customers?

Fortunately, Google offers a number of business tools that he used to let potential customers know about his new business. He was able to use AdWords (adwords.google.com/select/Login) to create ads that appeared in Google whenever someone searched for gourmet pet treats. By carefully selecting the right keywords (*dogs, treats,* and *cupcakes,* for instance) to use in the ad, he could help target his ad to reach the right audience. You get charged only when someone clicks on your ad, not for its display. Google helps keep the price down, too, which is great for a start-up business, by letting advertisers set a daily budget for the ad. AdWords also brought people to Michael's Web pages that he created with Google.

How? Michael created a Web site for The Corgi's Cupcake using Google Page Creator (www.pages.google.com), which is a free tool. Google hosted the Web pages he created there for free as well. He found it an easy tool to use. He could incorporate pictures of his cupcakes and video of some of his satisfied customers wolfing down some gourmet cupcakes.

He could also link to his blog, which he wrote using the "voice" of his corgi just for fun. But his corgi could also "speak" with authority about the quality of the doggie cupcakes too.

After he signed up for AdSense (www.google.com/adsense), Michael earned passive income from his Google Web pages. Google, you see, has an automated system that places ads on Web sites that are relevant to the content of the site. All he had to do was sign up for this free service. Google makes its money off AdSense from the advertisers who bid to put their ads on your Web pages.

Google also made it easier for Michael to process sales online with Google Checkout (checkout google.com/sell). There is also the potential for more sales. Google has found that customers click on ads 10% more when the ad displays the Google Checkout option. If you advertise with Google AdWords, some of your transactions will be free. For every dollar Michael spent on advertising with AdWords, he was able to process 10 dollars in sales for free the following month. For transactions after that, he was charged 20 cents per transaction. He didn't have to pay a setup fee, nor is there a monthly fee.

Naturally, Michael wanted a constant stream of dogs and their human pets (the ones with the pockets full of cash) to beat a path to his physical door as well as his Web site. But he could only afford to rent space for his shop in a building off the beaten path. How would local people and out-of-towners ever find him? The answer was Google Maps and its Local Business Center (www.google.com/local/add). Here he created a free listing that shows up in Google Maps whenever a customer is searching for dog treats available in his or her area. He created a free account, edited his listing whenever he needed to, and even added printable coupons to entice new customers.

With a great recipe for gourmet cupcakes for dogs and his knowledge and use of Google tools, Michael was able to get his business launched and to reach his market in a relatively short time.

USING GOOGLE TO SELL REAL ESTATE—LITTLE PALACES

George and his wife, Maddie, moved to a small town surrounded by countryside to retire. They'd both been in the real estate business for over twenty years in a large city. They were worn out from big-city stress, dealing with so many different kinds of residential listings, and driving in heavy traffic to show properties.

They had been living in their renovated small home for two years. They had fixed it up to not only meet their needs but to be their own "little palace" with some special touches such as French doors to a flagstone patio and a sunroom off the kitchen that they'd always wanted. After the hustle and bustle of the move and the renovation of their new home, they started feeling a little bored. They'd also spent more than they had intended for the renovations and had dipped into their savings.

They started to consider ideas of what they could do part-time that would help augment their income and that they would enjoy doing. They really didn't want to jump back into full-time real estate sales, especially since the market in their new town was very slow. There were a fair number of older, small homes on the market like theirs. Some were on the market because they'd been inherited but unwanted by out-of-town sons and daughters who had made new lives in other places and didn't want to return to their hometown and live in their childhood homes. Some had fallen into minor disrepair and weren't attractive starter homes because of the cost of fixing them up. They were priced below their value, but nobody was buying them.

While they were mulling over how to generate some income, George and Maddie got a call from a couple around their age, the Winslows, who had purchased a condo from them back in the city. They were looking for a small country home where they could retreat to from time to time and maybe eventually retire there. They wondered if George and Maddie could help them find a place. After chatting with them for a while, George and Maddie told them they'd call them back within a week.

As they discussed the Winslows's call, George and Maddie realized how much they'd enjoyed the process of fixing up their own little home. They'd met some reliable contractors who were skilled and fair in their pricing. They'd also gotten really good at using Google to search online for materials like antique fixtures and designer wallpaper for special touches that they couldn't find locally. They'd played around with Google's free three-dimensional modeling tool SketchUp (www.sketchup.google.com) to help them see how a part of the house might look if they took out a wall or put in a new window or added a sunroom. SketchUp allowed them to see how an idea might look and to decide if they really wanted it, because they couldn't afford all the customizations they dreamed up.

They also had a good time using Google's free blogger tool (www.blogger.com) to start a blog about the house renovation that their family, spread around the world, enjoyed reading and responding to on a regular basis. They posted photos of the progress on the blog as well.

Why not put all their new skills to work for clients who might want to find a small home and renovate and customize it as they did? They could specialize in helping out-of-town clients find and fix up small homes to become their own little palaces. Between what they had learned from fixing up their own home and what they had learned about some Google tools, it would be easy to work with people from a distance. They could use SketchUp to share ideas about renovations in 3-D. They could create a blog for each project to report on its progress and to post photos and to get feedback from their clients.

They could use Google Calendar (www.google.com/calendar), which could be shared with their clients on the Web, to record a time line for the renovations as well as site visits. Expenses could be recorded on Google Docs (www.docs.google.com) spreadsheets, and Google Docs could also be used to collaboratively work on the details of contracts because all parties could work within the same Web-based document.

George and Maddie talked it over for a few more days. Then they called the Winslows to see if they'd like to become their first clients in their new business, Little Palaces.

INCREASING PRODUCTIVITY—PARALEGAL BEAGLES

Jack started Paralegal Beagles five years ago in a large city in North Carolina. His business had grown rapidly based on the company's dedication to efficiency and speed in its provision of legal research. The company was now serving a dozen large law firms and many smaller ones.

Jack was concerned because his profit margin was shrinking even though business was booming. This was mainly due to the fact that he'd had to hire more people to keep up with demand. It took time to train the new hires to use the company's intranet to find the resources to do their jobs. This meant experienced employees were spending time training new employees instead of putting in billable hours. Furthermore, the company's database of information had become unwieldy as the company had grown, and even paralegals who had been with the company from its start were spending too much time trying to find information on it.

Jack started researching ways to remedy this problem. He looked at the business solutions that Google had to offer. The Google Search Appliance (www.google.com/enterprise/gsa) offered what he needed. It could crawl the content of the company's documents—220 different file types, including Microsoft documents, PDFs, and HTML—and create an index of them. Best of all, the user interface was the familiar Google search box that is easy to use. It was just like searching the Internet with Google, only it would be search Paralegal Beagle documents instead. It offered security and easy setup and maintenance as well.

Jack acquired the Google Search Appliance, and he was impressed with the results. Productivity increased because his paralegals could find what they needed quickly and easily. Considerably less time was spent training new hires. Some of his senior paralegals took the initiative to generate some best practices and tips that morphed over time into training modules for new employees that he licensed to other paralegal companies.

Jack researched other Google tools that might help his operation. He soon integrated the free tools of Google Calendar and Google Docs into the company. The company calendar that everyone could access on the Web was instrumental in keeping track of due dates for projects, meetings, vacations, and appointments. Google Docs helped with collaboration on team projects, because everyone on a team could access the documents they were drafting online.

Jack saw his profit margin climb again as a result of the Google Search Appliance and Google tools becoming part of his company. The paralegals spent less time searching and more time producing. Efficiency in collaboration improved with Google Docs and Google Calendar. Because more time was spent on billable hours rather than searching, he was able to ease back on hiring.

WRITING A GRANT PROPOSAL FOR
A COMMUNITY PILOT PROGRAM

Lateesha grew up in a poor county in the South. Her mother, Maria, had been a school teacher for 25 years, and Lateesha wanted to follow in her footsteps. Her mother had retired two years ago, just as Lateesha returned from college and started teaching at the same primary school she herself had attended and where her mother had taught while she was growing up.

Her mother had moved to a retirement home, a historic farm left to the county to be used by residents of the county. It housed 20 residents in the main house and its cottages. An endowment fund provided subsidies for residents who couldn't afford to pay the modest fee and who didn't have health insurance. Lateesha had wanted her mother to keep living at her childhood home with her, but her mother didn't want to be a burden and she had many friends at the retirement home.

Lateesha and a middle school teacher named Denzel had been working on a grant proposal most of the school year. They worked in schools in different parts of the county, so it had been easier to use Google Docs to work together on the draft since it was Web based and they could access it from any computer. They used Google search to find information to support their proposal and the spreadsheet that was part of Google Docs to work on their budget. Since chat was built into Google's Gmail, they could communicate in real time on their lunch breaks when they wanted to discuss ideas quickly.

Maria, working on one of two computers available to residents at the retirement home, helped them with the draft just as she had helped them brainstorm on their proposal. In their proposal, they asked for funds to develop a summer pilot program to address these community challenges:

1. The increasing number of elementary students who were at risk for failing to learn to read.
2. The high percentage of middle school students who were not reading on grade level and who struggled in content area textbooks, especially science.

3. Residents at the retirement home who had no family support, were isolated, and needed to feel they were still part of their community.

Lateesha, Maria, and Denzel planned a summer curriculum using Google tools. The daily schedule included the students and the retirees planning and then creating a small vegetable garden together in the morning. They planned to teach the students Google SketchUp to plan the layout of their garden. The garden and nature walks would provide real experiences around which they would plan science lessons.

They used iGoogle to centralize specific educational and organizational resources for the program that included a Google calendar and a collection of bookmarks of Web sites that had information related to vegetable gardening, nutritional value of vegetables, local weather, local wildlife, and native plants. Within iGoogle, they created a link to the program's blog that the students would write and illustrate with photos they would take and edit in Google's Picasa. They created Google spreadsheets to record weather, rainfall amounts, and soil temperatures.

In the afternoons, the older students would tutor the younger students in reading and read to them from books about nature, gardening, and weather gathered from the school library and from Google Book Search. Nature walks, in combination with what they learned from reading and working in their garden, would provide the stimulus for writing activities. Students would use Google blogger to inform their families and the community about the gardening project. They would add digital photos, using Google's Picasa to edit them. The younger children would use photos to illustrate their stories about nature walks. All of the retirees had agreed to donate an hour or two per day to help with the garden, the nature walks, and supporting the struggling readers during reading time.

With the help of Google tools, Lateesha, Denzel, and Maria were able to present a well-planned, well-integrated, and polished proposal to the private foundation that offered grants for educational projects. They used a laptop to show them the iGoogle site for the project and the beginning of the blog for the project. With these Google tools, they were able to make the project come to life so that the foundation committee could really see what they planned to do. The foundation awarded them the money they requested based on their curriculum that would integrate reading, science, and technology skills as well as serve different age groups in the community.

YOUTUBE TO STAY IN TOUCH AND GENERATE EXTRA MONEY

Colleen and her twin sister Bridget were inseparable growing up in Connemara, Ireland. They had gone to elementary school and high school together and then off to college together in Dublin. But after graduation, Colleen married an American who had taken his degree at her college. She returned to the States to live with him in Florida. Bridget went back to Connemara to work in a day care center. Within a year, she married her childhood sweetheart.

Colleen and Bridget missed each other terribly, and Colleen was homesick for Ireland. They wrote to each other regularly, but it wasn't until they discovered Gmail, with its capability of instant messaging, and YouTube that they really started to feel the distance between them diminish. They could stay in touch easier and for free. And YouTube let them share video about their daily lives.

Colleen and Bridget started a blog using Google's Blogger together with links to video snippets on YouTube comparing life in Florida with life in rural Ireland. Colleen posted videos she took of dolphins playing in the surf, the tropical birds, flowers, and trees that were so exotic compared to the landscape back home. She also posted a video-guided tour of sights to see and places to stay and eat in her town for friends and family who might want to visit.

Bridget posted blog entries with links to video describing and showing life in Connemara. She also provided information about local history, folklore, places to stay and eat, where to buy Irish crafts, and links to Irish music for Colleen's new friends in America to check out in case they wanted to plan a visit.

For a lark, the twins had signed up for Google AdSense and had Google Search added to their blog as well. Both were free and generated passive income if anyone clicked on the ads Google automatically generated relevant to their blog or used Google Search from their blog. Soon, ads related to the tourist trade for both Florida and Ireland appeared on their site. Between the two of them and their college friends and friends of friends, traffic to their site grew. The blog entries and videos were informative and often funny and provided an escape for people reading them during their work days. Bridget and Colleen answered questions from people they didn't know who had found their blog and who wanted know about life in their respective countries and the best times of year to vacation there and all kinds of questions they never anticipated.

After a year of carefully tending their blog and adding new video, the twins were surprised by how much passive income had been generated from AdSense. More than enough to pay for plane tickets so they could visit each other.

GOOGLE DOES IT ALL

Google has been more than generous by offering powerful but free and reasonably priced tools and services to small businesses to help them get started and to grow. Existing businesses can use some of these tools and products to solve problems that save them money and to help increase productivity. Google's design for ease of use makes these tools and services friendly to everyday computer users like you and me.

These scenarios give you an idea of how Google tools might be used to start or enhance a business. Companies of all sizes all over the world use AdWords to advertise products and services, and this is what generates most of Google's revenue. Individuals and companies also sign up for the free AdSense program that matches ads to Web sites' and blog pages' content. Google generates income from this program as well. So all you need is an idea and a little time to get acquainted with Google tools to play out your ideas for marketing a product, service, or knowledge.

Chapter Ten

Google Controversies

Like any company, Google has been involved in controversies during its short life. This chapter provides the background on some of these controversies so that you can consider the different points of view the public has taken in regard to them as well as Google's point of view. We'll also ask you, in the case of the China controversy, to assume the role of Google management to decide how to respond to the controversy. After you've had a chance to read the background and make your decision, we'll tell you how Google responded so that you can compare your management decision with that of Google's.

THE CHINA CONTROVERSY

A Chinese language version of Google has been available in China since 1999, the year Google was founded. Google offered this service from the United States and was not subject to direct regulation by the Chinese government. But Google learned in 2002 that it was, from time to time, not available to the Chinese people at all. There was some speculation that

---

Baidu

Baidu, China's leading search company, made its initial public offering of stock in the United States on August 5, 2005. Rumors that Google tried to buy the company before it went public possibly boosted the price of its shares on the first day it was sold. Baidu's stock price opened at $66—more than double its $27 initial offering price. At the end of the first day of trading, its price was $122. While Google didn't buy Baidu, it did have a 2.5% holding in the company. It sold this holding in June 2006. It acquired its shares for $5 million and sold them for more than $60 million.

Baidu, the Chinese company that dominates the search market in China, may have had some influence over the Chinese government to block Google completely.

Google also learned that many search queries were not making it through to Google's servers and that access overall was unreliable and slow. Sometimes, when Chinese users put in a search query, they were redirected to local Chinese search engines instead of the search request going to Google. Meanwhile, other U.S. companies like Yahoo! and Microsoft who compete with Google were starting operations from within China.

Google began doing research and reassessing its thinking about China. Google management was concerned that its service to end users in China did not meet Google's standards for efficiency and speed because the Chinese government was censoring search results, redirecting users to other search engines at times and at other times blocking access to Google completely. Google also believed that its mission to provide users access to the world's information was being compromised. Google's research about the situation led managers to talk to experts about the use of the Internet in China, human rights groups, government officials, as well as Google's Chinese employees in U.S. offices.

Google felt that the situation couldn't continue and that the company faced a choice. It could continue to do what it had been doing all along and just accept the fact that it couldn't meet its mission to deliver all of the available information it had to Chinese users. It would also have to accept the fact that Google service would at times be slow, inefficient, redirected, or blocked completely. Or Google could offer a new service from within China that would be subject to China's censorship and would also require compliance with the Chinese government's demand that Internet companies engage in self-censorship. Self-censorship, in general, required that it censor material that criticized the Chinese government, information about democracy and religion, and references to material about recent Tibetan uprisings, among other things. It was a tough decision.

Google didn't like offering service to users that didn't meet its standards. But, since China makes up one-fifth of the world's population and the popularity of the Internet was growing rapidly, China presents a huge potential market for advertising. Google's competitors were already making inroads into that market and so were Chinese companies. On the other hand, self-censorship was an affront not only to Google's commitment to "not doing evil," but to important U.S. democratic values such as free speech. Compromising those values would indirectly send the message to the Chinese government and the Chinese people that human rights violations could be overlooked. It would also send the message to the rest of the world that Google would compromise those values.

If you were Larry Page or Sergey Brin or another upper-level management person at Google, how would you have reacted? Please think about your response carefully before reading on to see how Google did respond.

GOOGLE'S DECISION

Google management decided to keep offering Google to China in the same format that it offered it to the rest of the world without censorship. It did this knowing that the same problems of censorship, poor service, redirection to Chinese companies, and complete loss of access would continue to occur. To offset that poor service, the company also began operations from within China and offered a new service that was self-censored and that would, like standard Google service, also be subject to censorship by the Chinese government. This service, while it would require taking out certain categories of information, would meet Google's standards for speed and efficiency. The strategic goal to gain market share in China would also have a better chance of being met.

Google's management made the decision based on its understanding of the context in which Google would be operating in China and how the Chinese end users of their service viewed the situation.

U.S. Congressman Chris Smith, chairman of a House subcommittee on human rights, called for a hearing to analyze the operating procedures of U.S. Internet companies in China. Elliot Schrage, vice president of global communications and public affairs for Google, testified before three separate subcommittees: Subcommittee on Asia and the Pacific, and the Subcommittee on Africa, Global Human Rights, and International Operations Committee on International Relations of the United States House of Representatives on February 15, 2006, about Google's decision to offer a censored version of Google.

Another Human Rights Controversy

Congressman James Leach (R-Iowa) alluded to another human rights controversy going on simultaneously to the China controversy in part of his statement made February 15, 2006, at the opening of a joint hearing on the Internet in China. This was, by the way, the same hearing in which Google was called to testify. His comment provides a context in which we can see that the U.S. government wasn't necessarily in a strong position to criticize China's human rights violations and to criticize companies for doing business with them. Here's what he said:

> This is a particularly awkward week for the United States to raise human rights concerns about another country given the

U.N. draft report on Guantanamo, as well as the continued ramifications of incidents at Abu Ghraib. But nonetheless, there are issues in U.S.-China relations that cannot be ducked, particularly when they involve the responsibilities of U.S. corporations.[1]

Congressman Leach was referring to the leak of a confidential draft report by a group of United Nations human rights investigators to several newspapers several days before the hearings on Internet companies and China. The report confirmed that, since January 2002, over 700 combatants and suspected terrorists captured in Afghanistan and elsewhere have been taken to the United States' Guantanamo Bay detention center. It also stated that two of the UN investigators concluded that the "legal regime applied to these detainees seriously undermines the rule of law and a number of fundamental universally recognized human rights, which are the essence of democratic societies."[2]

Schrage stated that Google had a business commitment to satisfy "the interests of users" and that this was the means by which Google had established its leadership and could maintain its leadership in its competitive industry. He went on to explain that it was Google's "policy conviction that expanding access to information to anyone who wants it will make our world a better, more informed, and freer place." In response to the restrictions that China and other governments impose on Google in meeting its business commitment and acting on its convictions, Google has had to become "responsive to local conditions."[3]

The belief that increasing the access to information to everyone will make the world a better place—Google's mission—is, oddly enough, itself a controversial issue because some argue that the Internet has helped terrorists disseminate information and recruit. But in China's case, many believe that, although free access without censorship would be preferable, the access that the Chinese have gained has changed their society in some positive ways. Aside from using the Internet to access information, young people are very active in blogs and chat rooms, and individuals are taking advantage of e-commerce. "From their perspective, the Internet—as filtered as it is—has already changed Chinese society profoundly. For the younger generation, especially, it has turned public speech into a daily act. This, ultimately, is the perspective that Google has adopted, too."[4]

In a *New York Times Magazine* article, Sergey told reporter Clive Thompson that, in making the decision about China, "revenue wasn't a big part of the equation...since it would be years before Google would make much if any profit in China." The Chinese search engine Baidu had already captured close to half of the search market in China, while Google's share was about one-quarter. Sergey, ever mindful of Google's mission, went on to say that their final decision "wasn't as much a business decision as a decision about getting people information."[5]

Google tried to work within the constraints of the Chinese government as best it could. It informed users whenever search results had to be removed because of censorship. It decided not to offer Gmail or Blogger within the new service that would result in personal information about Chinese users being stored on Chinese soil. In this way, Google would not be subject to demands from the Chinese government to turn over that information. Yahoo! was required to do this by the Chinese government, and it resulted in imprisonment for at least one of its users. Finally, Google has continued to offer its full service but from outside of China's borders, even though the Chinese government continues to censor it and at times block it completely.

Kai-Fu Lee, head of operations in China for Google believes that access to the Internet "will level the playing field for China's enormous rural underclass; once the country's small villages are connected...students thousands of miles from Shanghai or Beijing will be able to access online course materials from M.I.T. or Harvard and fully educate themselves."[6]

Elliot Schrage, in his testimony before the subcommittees, cited some research about the opinions of Chinese Internet users from what he called a "recent and well-respected study" by the Chinese Academy of Social Science. This research reveals more about how the Chinese view the power of the Internet to improve their society. First, 63% of Chinese Internet users believe that the Chinese will gain more knowledge about politics by going online. Over half of the Chinese Internet users believe that the Internet offers a forum for criticizing their government. And nearly half believe that the Internet presents the means to voice political points of view. Second, while the majority of the Chinese believe that violence and pornography should be censored on the Internet, less than 8% feel that content related to politics should be censored. Third, "by a 10:1 margin, Chinese Internet users believe that the Internet will make the world a better, rather than worse, place."[7]

Only time will tell the extent to which Google's China policy, as disappointing as it is to many Americans and worldwide advocates of free speech, has a positive influence on democratizing information and the Chinese society. And only time will tell whether this policy improves Google's market share in China.[8]

PRIVACY CONTROVERSIES: E-MAIL, RESIDENCY, AND HEALTH

Gmail

Google has been at the center of several significant privacy controversies. On April 1, 2004, it announced its launch of Gmail, a free

Internet-based e-mail service. Unlike the launch of most of its new products, Gmail from the outset would have relevant advertising embedded in it. Google planned to scan the content of users' e-mails and to insert relevant ads to the right-hand side of the e-mail just as it did when a user conducted a search on Google. Google needed more advertising space to meet demand, and this seemed like one good way to create that space.

Legislators, privacy advocates, and many individuals responded with outrage at the thought of their personal e-mails being invaded despite the fact that the e-mails would be scanned to match the ads with the content of the e-mails by computers, not by humans. The ferocity of the reaction indicates the extent to which e-mail is considered a totally private sphere by those who use it and, perhaps, the general climate of uneasiness that had been growing over time about privacy on the Internet. Obviously, the most obvious solution for those who objected to Gmail would be to simply not sign up to use it with Google. This was a choice any individual could make—no one was forced to use this free e-mail service.

The furor did prompt Google to make its privacy policies about all of its services quite clear on its Web site, including Gmail. Losing potential Gmail users and the advertising that might be sold was serious. But equally serious was the possibility of breaching the trust of Google users that the company had spent the years since its inception trying to build.

Google explains that it "provide[s] advertisers only aggregated non-personal information such as the number of times one of their ads was clicked." Except as required by law, Google does not share or sell personal information.[9]

In the frequently asked questions section of its extensive Web site on its privacy policy (www.google.com/privacy_faq.html), the company answers a question about the nature of "protections" individuals have "against intrusions by the government" related to using Google. Google responds that it "does comply with valid legal process, such as search warrants, court orders, or subpoenas seeking personal information." To be a law-abiding company, this is what Google must do. And don't we expect companies to abide by the law? At the same time, it's understandable that many people are uneasy about the information stored in Gmail (if they signed up for it). The information required to register for it combined with the history of searches that Google stores can represent an extraordinary amount of personal information for any company to have on record, even if it promises not to sell it or share it unless compelled to do so by law.[10]

The Privacy of Where We Live

The fact that Google makes information about where we live available to anyone seeking that information through search, Google Maps, and Google Earth makes many people feel vulnerable. Type in someone's phone number and you can get a map to where he or she lives. Type in someone's name and you can get his or her address and phone number. Type in an address in Google Maps in San Francisco, New York, Las Vegas, Denver, and Miami and you can use an option to get a street-level view of the address. The capacity of Google Earth to display satellite images of buildings and streets in detail has also alarmed some governments, including the U.S. government, for security reasons.

The Privacy of Health Our Health Records

Many of us worry about the security and privacy of our health records that are maintained as hard copies. Will they be lost? Will they be misfiled? Who has access to them? Will information be written legibly so that other doctors can read it? Has all the information in them been entered accurately? How can we get up-to-date copies of our records from all the doctors we might see if we move? Somehow this vital and highly personal information seems out of our control. Depending on one's point of view, this situation may improve or worsen with the move toward electronic health records.

In 2004, President Bush set the goal that most Americans would have electronic medical records by 2014. He maintained that meeting this goal would improve the quality of health care, reduce its cost, help prevent medical errors, increase administrative efficiency, and promote access to affordable health care. Patient participation would be voluntary. The design behind the electronic records would ensure privacy and the secure transmission of records between health care providers only when authorized by the patient.[11]

In February 2008, Google responded to Bush's goal. It announced that Google Health was in development. The competition to create the online technology to meet the president's goal was, however, already underway before Google made its announcement. Microsoft and Revolution Health Group LLC have already launched Web sites for personal health records. To date, people have been slow to use any of them, partly because only 14% of medical practices in the United States keep records electronically, which makes transferring them to an online repository difficult, if not impossible.

Prior to the formal announcement of its program, Google announced a pilot project with Cleveland Clinic, a nonprofit medical center. While the clinic already keeps records online in a private system, administrators believe that having a system on Google will facilitate the ability of medical providers outside the clinic to add data about patients and add to the portability of their patients' health records. The Cleveland pilot project is by invitation only to some of the clinic's patients. It will help Google test the security of its system as well as its ease of use.

Online personal health records are the responsibility of the patient to compile if their health provider doesn't have them already online. Aside from information such as insurance information and emergency contacts, users can enter their family medical history, information about allergies, what prescriptions they take and other information about their medical conditions, which doctors they see, and their contact information. Because the information is on the Web, with the patient's consent, it could be accessed by an emergency room, for example, upon a patient's admission to the hospital. Vital information about the patient could potentially be instantaneously available.

The drive to put personal medical information online has merit. Lives could be saved by it. It also represents an enormous new source of revenue for Google and its competitors. But for many, the same nagging doubts about the security and privacy of the current paper-based system remains. How private and secure would the information really be?

COPYRIGHT CONTROVERSIES

The copyright controversies into which Google has been drawn include those related to the Google Print Program and YouTube. These controversies seemed inevitable given Google's commitment to collecting and indexing as much of the world's information as possible and the fact that no one had previously engaged in such a task on the universal scale Google is attempting.

The Google Print Program

The Google Book Search (books.google.com/googlebooks/about. html) includes separate programs for publishers and for libraries. The Google Publisher Program (books.google.com/partner) is a collaboration with book publishers to make it easy for people to search for titles and to buy them. Ads on the search result pages are optional. Google says that most of the revenue from this program goes to the publishers.

The Google Books Library Project (books.google.com/googlebooks/ library.html) has generated controversy from the beginning. In 2005, the program was born of agreements with the university libraries of Harvard, Stanford, the University of Michigan, and the University of Oxford as well as the New York Public Library. The program was renamed Google Book Search in late fall 2005. The University of California, the University of Wisconsin, the University of Virginia, and the Universidad Complutense de Madrid joined in 2006. The Princeton University library and the University of Texas at Austin joined in 2007.

In collaboration with these libraries, Google scans books in the public domain as well as in-copyright books. For the books still under copyright, Google only displays information much like a card catalog displays in a library and includes only enough text from the book to enable someone to confirm that this is the book sought. Google's goal is to create an index of all the books in the world that can be searched using Google. It also intends to scan out-of-print books in their entirety, which benefits individuals searching for books that may be impossible to find.

The library program caused an uproar from its beginning in the publishing community and soon received a lot of press. Google perceived that much of the uproar was a result of an inadequate or inaccurate understanding of the issues. Aside from what it said about the controversy in interviews, it also published a Facts and Fiction page on its Web site (books. google.com/googlebooks/newsviews/facts_fiction.html) about the situation to try to clarify what the company was actually doing. The company first presents the "fiction" that might be pervasive in the press and public thinking and then counters it with the "fact."

In response to the fiction that the company is offering every book in the world free to Google users to download, it notes that only full versions of books out of copyright are available. Books still in copyright have a bibliographic reference, a snippet from the book to ensure the identity of the work, and links to where it can be bought or borrowed.

In response to the fiction that Google is displaying whole pages rather than snippets and therefore must be infringing on copyright law, Google again assures readers that only full pages from books out of copyright are displayed.

In response to the fiction that booksellers pay Google to include links on Google Book Search, Google responds with the fact that it provides links to make it easier for people to find a place to buy the book they are seeking and for publishers to market their books. Those selling books don't pay to have their links included, and Google doesn't make any money when a book is sold by a retailer such as Amazon.

Google counters the fiction that it's generating revenue from advertising on Google Book Search and denying income to copyright holders by noting that the company doesn't put an ad on a book's page unless the publisher wants an ad on the page and has given Google permission to do so. It states that "the majority of the revenue is given back to the copyright holder. In other words, we profit from Google Book Search ads only to the extent that our publishing partners do as well."[12]

Many publishers challenge Google's right to copy and index copyrighted works even if the full text of copyrighted works is not made available, only bibliographic information. Google believes that what it is doing is legal under the fair use provision of copyright law. It also gives publishers the right to opt out of the program so that their books scanned in participating libraries will not be made available to Google users. Some publishers feel that being given the option to opt out after their books are scanned and available on Google puts an unfair burden on them to negotiate opting out of the program after the fact. Several publishers and organizations have taken Google to court over these issues, claiming that Google has violated the fair use provision of U.S. copyright law. Fair use on such a huge scale hasn't been tested in the courts.

Fair Use

The U.S. Code below from Title 17, Chapter 1, is the section of U.S. law that is relevant to the question of whether Google is in violation of copyright law.

§ 107. Limitations on exclusive rights: Fair use

Notwithstanding the provisions of sections 106 and 106A, the fair use of a copyrighted work, including such use by reproduction in copies or phonorecords or by any other means specified by that section, for purposes such as criticism, comment, news reporting, teaching (including multiple copies for classroom use), scholarship, or research, is not an infringement of copyright. In determining whether the use made of a work in any particular case is a fair use the factors to be considered shall include:

1. the purpose and character of the use, including whether such use is of a commercial nature or is for nonprofit educational purposes;
2. the nature of the copyrighted work;
3. the amount and substantiality of the portion used in relation to the copyrighted work as a whole; and
4. the effect of the use upon the potential market for or value of the copyrighted work.

The fact that a work is unpublished shall not itself bar a finding of fair use if such finding is made upon consideration of all the above factors.[13]

Ralph Oman, a lawyer and former register of copyrights for the U.S. Copyright Office, explained the threat to publishers from its point of view: "Publishers get extremely nervous when there is a digital copy of something floating around in cyberspace forever. One copy out there is enough to destroy the economic value of a work, and the damage that can be done is so much greater."[14]

Google sees its effort as part of its mission to make all the information in the world available to everyone. It believes that there is a benefit both to people seeking books and to publishers. And it provides testimonials on its Web site (books.google.com/googlebooks/newsviews/pub.html) from publishers who are partners in the program who seem to agree with the company.

Ed Crutchely, book sales director for Blackwell's, states on the site that, "A 1999 Blackwell's title, *Metaphysics: An Anthology,* has had 2,583 pageviews and 597 'buy this book' click-throughs since it became part of the program. Without any other marketing, the title has had its best year in the US since publication... the high rate of 'buy this book' clicks is translating into sales for our deep backlist."[15]

Brian Murray, HarperCollins Group president explained the rather dramatic difference between traffic on its site for one of its titles and the amount of traffic to the book on Google's site once it was part of the program for publishers: "Google has delivered more than six million page views for HarperCollins in 16 months. On average, each title has had 97 page views. Murray pointed to *Mere Christianity,* by C. S. Lewis, listed on the [HarperCollins] website, where it has had 351 page views and 14 'buy this book' clicks. On Google, the same title has had 15,641 page views and 284 click-throughs."[16]

Click-throughs

What is a "click-through"? In the context that Brian Murray is using the term, it refers potential customers clicking on the link to go to the publisher's site, where they will be able to buy the book if they choose to do so.

Viacom's Lawsuit against Google over Video

While other entertainment and media producers have sued Google and others may do so in the future, Viacom's suit against Google will be a landmark case. Viacom sued Google and its subsidiary, YouTube, in federal court on March 14, 2007, claiming copyright infringement that denied individuals financial compensation for their contribution to the videos shown on YouTube. Viacom is the parent company of MTV and Comedy Central. Viacom is asking for more than $1 billion in damages. Legal experts expect the case to be in the courts for several years before it is resolved.

Google acquired YouTube in October 2007. It expected legal battles and set aside money to fund them when they happened. Google has been in the process of completing deals with other entertainment companies, including the BBC, Warner Music Group, and CBS. Some observers believe that Viacom's lawsuit is a reflection of Viacom's frustration about trying to negotiate with Google. The previous month, Viacom had requested that Google remove 100,000 clips owned by Viacom and Google did comply. But a CNET News.com article quoted an anonymous source inside Viacom as saying that Viacom "would likely have not filed suit, had it not repeatedly found clips that it had already asked to be taken down." Furthermore, the same source said that "The company basically is paying for an entire new department to watch YouTube."[17] Viacom and other media companies believe that it is an unfair burden for them to have to monitor YouTube to find out whether their material is being used.

Google's statement in response to the lawsuit was that it was "confident that YouTube has respected the legal rights of copyright holders. We will certainly not let this suit become a distraction to the continuing growth and strong performance of YouTube."[18]

In October 2007, Google finally introduced an antipiracy tool that it had been working on even before it acquired YouTube. In order for the tool to work, owners of copyrighted material must submit copies of their videos to YouTube that they want to protect. The antipiracy tool analyzes all video as it is uploaded to YouTube to see whether there is a match with its database of copyrighted material submitted by content owners. Google expects to keep working on the tool to improve it over time.

Google is taking some risks to increase the number, nature, and extent of its markets. It is also an innovator offering new services as it attempts to meet its mission. With the China controversy, it is risking its reputation for not doing evil. The privacy and copyright controversies risk its reputation in the same way and subject it to legal action. Google is not likely to be deterred from taking risks in the future by the fallout from the controversies in which it's currently involved. It has to take chances to survive, to grow, and to meet its mission, and it has more than adequate resources to fund its legal battles.

NOTES

1. http://www.america.gov/st/washfile-english/2006/February/2006021515 4055ASesuarK0.9963648.html (accessed May 1, 2008).

2. Colum Lynch, "U.N. Draft Decries U.S. on Detainee Treatment," *Washington Post,* February 14, 2006, http://www.washingtonpost.com/wp-dyn/content/article/2006/02/13/AR2006021301848.html (accessed April 19, 2008).

3. Karen Wickre, "Testimony: The Internet in China," The Official Google Blog, February 15, 2006, http://googleblog.blogspot.com/2006/02/testimony-internet-in-china.html (accessed April 29, 2008).

4. Clive Thompson, "Google's China Problem (and China's Google Problem)," *New York Times,* April 23, 2006, http://www.nytimes.com/2006/04/23/magazine/23google.html?pagewanted=1&ei=5090&en=972002761056363f&ex=1303444800 (accessed April 27, 2008).

5. Ibid.

6. Ibid.

7. Karen Wickre, "Testimony: The Internet in China," The Official Google Blog, February 15, 2006, http://googleblog.blogspot.com/2006/02/testimony-internet-in-china.html (accessed April 29, 2008).

8. Clive Thompson, "Google's China Problem (and China's Google Problem)," *New York Times,* April 23, 2006, http://www.nytimes.com/2006/04/23/magazine/23google.html?pagewanted=1&ei=5090&en=972002761056363f&ex=1303444800 (accessed April 27, 2008).

9. "Gmail: Google's Approach to Email," http://gmail.google.com/mail/help/privacy.html (accessed May 1, 2008).

10. "Google Privacy FAQ," Google Privacy Center, http://www.google.com/privacy_faq.html (accessed April 26, 2008).

11. "Promoting Innovation and Competitiveness: President Bush's Technology Agenda—A New Generation of American Innovation," The White House, Policies in Focus, http://www.whitehouse.gov/infocus/technology/economic_policy 2004 04/chap3.html (accessed April 30, 2008).

12. "Google Book Search: News & Views—Facts & Fiction," Google Book Search, http://books.google.com/googlebooks/newsviews/facts_fiction.html (accessed April 24, 2008).

13. "Copyright Law of the United States of America and Related Laws Contained in Title 17 of the *United States Code,* U.S. Copyright Office, http://www.copyright.gov/title17/92chap1.html#107 (accessed May 2, 2008).

14. Elinor Mills, "Google's Battle over Library Books," CNET News.com, October 24, 2005, http://www.news.com/Googles-battle-over-library-books/2100-1025_3-5907506.html (accessed April 25, 2008).

15. "Google Book Search: News & Views—Publisher Case Studies," Google Book Search, http://books.google.com/googlebooks/newsviews/pub.html (accessed May 5, 2008).

16. Ibid.

17. Anne Broache and Greg Sandoval, "Viacom Sues Google over YouTube Clips," CNET News.com, March 13, 2007, http://www.news.com/Viacom-sues-Google-over-YouTube-clips/2100-1030_3-6166668.html (accessed May 2, 2008).

18. Jeremy W. Peters, "Viacom Sues Google over YouTube Video Clips," *New York Times,* March 14, 2007, http://www.nytimes.com/2007/03/14/business/14viacom.web.html (accessed May 3, 2008).

Chapter Eleven

The Future of Google

While softened by humor, the following quote from Google's corporate Web page points to the reality of the evolution of the company's mission over time. It is inevitable that Google's mission manifests in new ways as it interacts with its users to meet their evolving needs and as it responds defensively to shifts in its competitive environment. At the same time, it has to make offensive moves to maintain its dominance in search and online advertising as well as explore and expand into new potentially revenue-rich territory.

> Over time we've expanded our view of the range of services we can offer—web search, for instance, isn't the only way for people to access or use information—and products that then seemed unlikely are now key aspects of our portfolio. This doesn't mean we've changed our core mission; just that the farther we travel toward achieving it, the more those blurry objects on the horizon come into sharper focus (to be replaced, of course, by more blurry objects).[1]

Some market analysts as well as business academicians question whether Google is losing its focus and whether that poses a risk to its future. Vinton Cerf, who holds the position of vice president and Internet evangelist at Google responded to an interview question about Google's loss of focus that seemed to divert it from its original mission:

> The focus isn't simply on search. The focus is on making information discoverable and useful, so all of these things you see happening at Google are side effects of expanding on the original paradigm, which was making search an effective tool. Now we're looking at how to make other information activities more effective and relevant.[2]

Vinton Cerf

Vice President and Chief Internet Evangelist for Google

Vinton Cerf, with Robert Kahn, was instrumental in the development of the TCP/IP protocols and basic architecture of the Internet. They received the U.S. Presidential Medal of Freedom in 2005—the highest civilian honor given in the United States—in recognition of their work as leaders in the "digital revolution that has transformed global commerce, communication, and entertainment."

Before coming to Google, Cerf worked for the U.S. Department of Defense's Advanced Research Projects Agency from 1976 to 1982. From 1982 to 1986, he was vice president of MCI and senior vice president from 1994 to 2005. He has been a visiting scientist at the Jet Propulsion Laboratory since 1998.

Well recognized for his lifetime achievements and wearing three-piece suits, Cerf helps Google to identify "new enabling technologies and applications on the Internet and other platforms."[3]

To get a sense of where Google is going, it's helpful to look at its past and current trends to see which strategies have generated revenue streams that have flowed steadily and grown for the company. These are strategies it is likely to continue. We can also consider some recent initiatives and where they might lead. But future courses of action for any company are, to some extent, unpredictable. Add to that the fact that Google loves secrecy and considers it a strategic tool, and the crystal ball into which we gaze to try to determine Google's future gets murkier. Like all companies and other living entities, it is subject to fate—those components of its environment that it can't control, such as world events, the weather, and the moves of competitors.

But unless Larry and Sergey change radically, we can safely assume the core mission of Google will remain the same, though perhaps reinterpreted, as long as they are at the helm, and we can also assume there will be some surprises that will make it all very exciting to watch unfold. Given that Google has the largest computing system in the world with a mammoth index of Web-based information and the capacity to transfer that search capability to other large organizations, it will be interesting to see how its projects with NASA go and what other partnerships might evolve with governments and global organizations.

Google has spent millions of dollars on research in recent years. It is likely to continue to be an exemplary think tank around critical issues related to search and making the world's information available through different media. The 20% time that its engineers are required to spend on research that interests them has yielded some great products for Google users and new revenue streams for Google. It also has strong relationships with the global community of software engineers who contribute valuable feedback on products introduced through Google Labs and who experiment with Google open-source code and new applications. It has assembled, and seems likely to continue to attract, some of the smartest people in the world to conduct this kind of research. But can we be sure that it can keep attracting talent? Can Google maintain its productive corporate culture? Can it maintain its popularity with the searchers?

VARIATIONS ON AN ADVERTISING THEME

Google's biggest source of revenue to date has been the sale of Web-based advertising. To bolster its advertising revenue stream even more, it can use several tactics. It can sell more Web-based ads connected to search to more advertisers worldwide. It also can sell more ads for placement within other kinds of media such as Web-based video and wireless devices. And it can diversify the kinds of ads that it sells, which might open new markets for them.

Maintaining its position as the number one search engine in the world based on volume of users will continue to help the volume of its Web-based ads to grow. Since it continues to research ways to improve the relevance of its search results and to return them quickly, it seems likely to continue to attract more users for search. More advertisers are likely to join the Google advertising program as long as it remains the number one search destination and continues to place ads on relevant pages for users. Advertisers want to place ads where there is the most traffic, and targeting an audience that is likely to buy their products brings them a higher return on their advertising dollars.

In April 2007, Google reported that it would pay $3.1 billion for the advertising company DoubleClick. Initially, Google's willingness to pay this price caused some consternation in the business world, because it seemed to be too high. But Google had been competing with Microsoft for DoubleClick. The acquisition was strategically important to Google for several reasons. On March 11, 2008, the deal was completed.

The acquisition of DoubleClick will help Google to advance toward its goal of diversification into display ads. Over the course of more than a decade, DoubleClick developed a successful online display ad program and software to help its clients increase their revenue from ads. They built strong relationships with many online publishers such as America Online, MySpace, Time Warner's *Sports Illustrated*, Viacom's MTV Networks, and the *Wall Street Journal* and about half of the existing online ad agencies. Time Warner's AOL and MySpace are two of the most popular destinations on the Web. With the acquisition of DoubleClick, Google now has the rights to provide search ads on both sites. Much of DoubleClick's advertising is for promotion purposes rather than sales, but companies pay handsomely for those kinds of ads to keep their brand name in front of the public.[4]

Google and Microsoft were in a bidding war to acquire DoubleClick. Microsoft's failure to acquire the company will slow its effort to catch up with Google in the online advertising market. That fact makes the acquisition for Google even more valuable. And with DoubleClick, Google is looking at the potential to steadily increase its revenues from the new source of display ads. Google owns around two-thirds of the search advertising market. It accounted for $6.76 billion of online ad spending in 2006 and was projected by eMarketer to grow to $10.3 billion by 2010. Display advertising accounted for $3.34 billion in 2006 and is expected by 2010 to reach $10.3 billion.[5]

GOOGLE'S COMMITMENT TO VIDEO CONTINUES

Google views video, like print and images, as another form of information that it wants to make available to the world. It is also another medium for which it can sell ads.

Google's commitment to video has been obvious for some time. On Google Video, you can search from a collection of millions of indexed videos that include movie clips, documentaries, TV shows, and music videos. When you type in a search term in the Google Video search box, Google puts the same powerful search engine to work to return the highly relevant results we've come to expect from our searches with Google for printed material.

Google's ongoing commitment to video continued with its acquisition of YouTube in 2006, just a year after YouTube was officially launched. In its short life, YouTube quickly became the premier destination for users to share and view original videos globally on the Web. It also allows people to share video through a variety of ways—on Web sites, blogs, e-mail, and mobile devices. Just as blogs enabled everyone to share their thoughts in print, YouTube empowers people to become video producers and to make their movies, whether informational or creative, available to the world. YouTube also has partnerships with professional producers of video such as CBS, the BBC, and Warner Music Group.[6]

YouTube provides another opportunity for advertisers to take advantage of Google's ability to provide targeted ads based on its search technology on a massive global scale. It's a way for Google to increase its income from Web-based advertising.

Google wisely left YouTube's cofounders Chad Hurley and Steve Chen in place as chief executives and gave them considerable autonomy as a subsidiary of Google to continue what they were already doing so well. YouTube was a savvy acquisition for Google in terms of increasing different kinds of content for advertising space that it could offer to existing and new advertisers and a good fit for its mission. It was also very smart to keep YouTube out of the hands of Google's competitors.

THE WIRELESS MARKET

Google wants to reach the wireless market more effectively and more thoroughly. Mobile phones are used by 3 billion people worldwide and that number will continue to grow. Currently, the sales of portable technology are exceeding the sales of personal computers. Market analysts project that the revenue potential from targeted ads to match search queries from smart phones could exceed the revenue generated by advertising on computer-based search. Google is better positioned than its competitors to provide this kind of effective advertising tied to search.

One of its significant early moves toward wireless was Google's 1995 acquisition of a young company named Android, Inc. that was developing software for mobile phones. Andy Rubin, an Android cofounder, is currently Google's director of mobile platforms.

In November 2007, the Open Handset Alliance, a multinational group of 34 technology and wireless companies, issued a press release to announce its collaboration to develop Android, "the first complete, open, and free mobile platform." The alliance includes Google, T-Mobile, Qualcomm, and Motorola, among others.[7]

The goal of the alliance is to give consumers a better mobile phone experience than what is currently available. To reach this goal, the alliance created a collaborative development environment based on open-source software. Within this environment, it hopes to accelerate the process of bringing innovative products to the consumer and at a much lower cost and to create an alternative to the proprietary platforms of Microsoft and Symbian.

The Android mobile software stack includes an operating system, an HTML browser, middleware, and applications. Making this software available to developers gives them the freedom to customize Android. The alliance isn't envisioning just one smart phone—that the press was inclined to dub "the Google phone"—coming out of this development process, but rather many different kinds of mobile devices.

A week after the November 2007 press conference, Google announced the Android Developer Challenge that consists of $10 million in cash prizes ranging from $25,000 to $275,000 to be awarded to developers who build mobile applications for Android selected by a panel of judges made up of members of the Open Handset Alliance. The Alliance provided the potential developers with the Android software developer kit. While the Google Web site for the Android Developer Challenge (www. code.google.com/android/adc.html) invites developers to build their favorite mobile application, suggestions were made for areas of focus that include social networking, media consumption, management, editing, sharing, productivity, collaboration such as e-mail and instant messaging, gaming, and news and information.[8]

What does all this mean for Google? The Android platform gives Google the potential to make the most out of some of its applications like Gmail and Google Maps on smart mobile devices as well as reach more markets with its advertising model. Also, because the Android software is free, it is likely to affect the profits of competitors whose installation of their operating systems is not free. Prices of smart phones could come down too, because manufacturers won't have to pay for software.

GETTING ON THE AIR WAVES

With Android likely to be available in the second half of 2008, Google needed to solve the problem of the restrictions major U.S. mobile carriers AT&T and Verizon placed on which handsets and Internet services could be used on their networks. The best handset and software in the world doesn't do anybody any good if they can't use it. The control of these carriers was a significant barrier to Google's increasing its market share of Web-based advertising on mobile phones. One possible solution was to bid on part of the U.S. mobile telecoms spectrum being auctioned by the U.S. government. The Federal Communications Commission (FCC) was conducting the auction of signal spectrum to be opened up as part of the nationwide conversion to digital television signals schedule for 2009. The spectrum offered the potential to create a new wireless broadband Internet service. Early in the process, it seemed that whoever submitted the winning bid would control this potential.

The approaching auction stirred a robust debate between advocacy groups—who favored open competition that would allow new entrants who might bring innovation, lower prices, and increased Internet access for rural areas and small communities—and the giants AT&T and Verizon—who planned to bid and, if successful, would continue to control how the public would access the Internet and the quality and nature of the experience.

Free Press campaign director Timothy Karr, in a solicitation letter to members of the Save the Internet Coalition who advocated for net neutrality, wrote:

[T]he United States has fallen to 16th in the world in high-speed Internet rankings, with few choices and some of the highest prices for the slowest speeds in the world. We will continue this decline as long as we let AT&T, Verizon and Comcast dictate the terms of Internet access for the majority of Americans.[9]

The coalition sent the FCC over 230,000 signatures in June 2007 in support of using the spectrum for public wireless broadband.

Jumping into the debate, Google's legal campaign was led by Richard Whitt, former head of the regulatory department for MCI, formerly known as WorldCom and now owned by Verizon. Google made its position clear in a July 9, 2007, ex parte filing made by Whitt with the FCC when it proposed that four conditions be placed on the winner(s) of the bidding process for the 700-MHz spectrum.

1. Those providing service based on the new spectrum would not limit the ability of end users to download and use software applications of their choice on their mobile phones.
2. End users should be able to use handsets of their choice with the new wireless network. Google argued that an "open devices environment improves consumer choice—and facilitates full competition—by allowing users then to utilize the device of their choosing, on the network of their choosing."[10]
3. Third-party wireless providers should be able to acquire wireless service on a wholesale basis for resale at commercially reasonable rates. Google noted that this provision would create opportunities for smaller businesses to resell wireless services.
4. The fourth provision Google requested was open networks that would allow Internet Service providers (ISPs) to connect their network facilities with the wireless providers' last mile towers.

Google also asked that the FCC enforce these rules if they adopted them. They noted that their overall intention with their request that the FCC place these conditions on the winner of the auction was to ensure consumer choice and to create the conditions necessary for a genuine third-party broadband platform that would stimulate competition.

In the same filing, Google revealed that it had been engaged in meetings with auction experts as well as creating game theory scenarios with experts to decide whether to participate in the auction and, if it participated, how to do so successfully. Google realized as a result of its research and analysis, as stated in its filing, that the incumbent wireless carriers (AT&T and Verizon) were likely to win the bidding process. Google went on explain why actually winning the bidding process would not necessarily be to Google's economic advantage.

Simply put, large incumbents have significant built-in advantages that are very difficult to overcome. While some argue that Google could simply choose to outbid any single entity in the auction, the notion of "deep pockets" alone is not the correct measure in this particular instance. Instead, the decisive factors include other significant economic and operational barriers to entry, and the relative value and usefulness of spectrum to the bidders. In particular, Verizon and AT&T are well-established, vertically-integrated incumbent providers of wireless and wireline services. By contrast, Google is a Web-based software applications company, not a service provider, with little pertinent experience in the wireless market and no legacy business models to protect. The incumbent carriers have an embedded national network of towers, backhaul, customers, retail outlets, and advertising. The incumbents also have far more ready cash flow at hand, and the willingness to spend it in furtherance of existing business plans. Consequently, the spectrum simply has more economic value and overall usefulness to incumbents like Verizon or AT&T, than to a would-be new entrant like Google.[11]

So, even at this early stage of the game, Google was probably more interested in influencing the outcome of how the new spectrum could be used by third-parties post auction rather than winning the bid for the spectrum. Winning would have advantages in terms of simplifying its access to and use of the spectrum, but it would bring tremendous additional costs to build the structure it described in the excerpt from its ex parte filing to use it.

AT&T and Verizon's response to the filing was to threaten to withdraw from the auction if open access was mandated, which would have left the FCC unable to raise cash it wanted from the sale of the spectrum.

Philosophically, Google's management agreed with the point of view of the citizen advocacy groups that wanted more competition. It was in keeping with its overall support over the years of open-source solutions that foster innovation and competition, as well as its most recent formation of the Open Handset Alliance.

But, at the same time, for its own strategic purposes to increase revenue, it wanted to be sure that its search services and its advertisers would be able to find a new home without barriers on the new wireless spectrum. Google could reach a much larger audience worldwide if this happened. At this point in time, Google is working on Android and working with EarthLink to provide free WiFi wireless broadband in San Francisco. It had also joined a consortium called the Coalition for 4G, which included eBay, Yahoo, Intel, DirectTV, Access Spectrum, and EchoStar. Prior to Google's July ex parte filing, the coalition had sent letters to the FCC to lobby for how it wanted the auction conducted.

Google did bid in the auction that took place in February 2008 and, by doing so, jacked the bidding up over the $4.6 billion that was required to trigger some of the provisions that it had asked for in its ex parte filing. Verizon won most of the C block of the spectrum and will be required to allow the use of all mobile devices. This opened the door for Google's Android software to gain wider use over time. Google got what it wanted without having to spend more than $10 billion to buy and build a wireless network had they won the auction.

Google congratulated Verizon in a statement that also declared the outcome of the auction to be a victory for consumers. It stated that consumers can look forward to getting more out of their use of mobile phones and wireless devices. No doubt, Google plans to help consumers get more out of their wireless experience by offering them the Android software in mobile phones and devices produced by current and future partners.

PUSHING FOR MORE AIRWAVES

Hardly taking time to catch its breath after the big auction, Google joined forces with Microsoft, Royal Philips Electronic, Dell, and Intel in a coalition called the White Spaces Coalition to propose a plan to the FCC that would let wireless Internet devices make use of vacant television airwaves after TV broadcasters change over to digital signals in 2009. The White Spaces Coalition stated that this would increase Internet access for people in the United States and take advantage of TV white spaces, of which only 5% are used.[12]

Google played a leadership role in the formation of this alliance, indicating again its commitment to opening the airwaves any way it can for wireless devices that could operate on its Android software and giving users easy access to search and new ways to reach mobile users with ads tied to search.

GOOGLE'S ACQUISITIONS, PARTNERSHIPS, AND ALLIANCES

Google has used acquisitions adeptly for strategic purposes and to increase revenue. Sometimes the acquisitions, like Pyra Labs, which created Blogger, are easily and quickly offered to the public as Google entities for immediate use. Other times, the new acquisitions are taken into Google for additional work before becoming public. But, to date, acquisitions such as Upstartle (which produced an online word processor prior to sale and later became the basis of Google Docs and Spreadsheets), YouTube, and DoubleClick, among others, have been good investments. YouTube and DoubleClick brought the possibility of significant revenue increases. They were also valuable companies to deny competitors.

Google's early partnerships with AOL and Yahoo! benefited both partners. It has continued to successfully partner with industry giants and, more recently, NASA. In 2005, Google announced a partnership with NASA Ames Research Center to build a research center and to collaborate on projects related to the entrepreneurial space industry, distributed computing, nanotechnology, and large-scale data management. In 2006, it entered into a $900 million agreement to provide search and advertising on the social networking site, MySpace, owned by News Corp.'s Fox Interactive Media.[13]

In March 2008, Google, Yahoo!, Engage.com, Friendster, hi5, Hyves, imeem, LinkedIn, Ning, Oracle, orkut, Plaxo, Salesforce.com, Six Apart,

Tianji, Viadeo, and XING, among others, announced their formation of the OpenSocial Foundation. As a nonprofit, the OpenSocial Foundation advocates that social network applications, which have always been community-driven, will remain open and free. Social networks, regardless of who owns them, all benefit from using the same open code for innovation and for the dissemination of tools and services across all social network sites.[14]

To make progress in the realm of wireless, Google has helped to form powerful alliances that joined together to create a collaborative development environment and to lobby the FCC.

Google depends on collaboration to stimulate innovation and productivity in its own shop. Larry and Sergey are committed to teamwork both within the Googleplex and, to the extent that it serves their interests, collaboration within the industry. They also recognize that competition is also inevitable and necessary in order for them to meet Google's mission and that it's a way to push them and their competition to develop better products and services.

Google's continued financial success depends on its ability to retain the loyalty of its users, which makes it the number one search destination. By maintaining and growing this customer base globally and increasing the media through which it reaches them, it hopes to be able to continue to attract the advertising dollars that generate most of its revenue. To date, it has been able to attract talented and dedicated engineers and to acquire companies that enable it to improve its products and anticipate what users want in new services and products.

EXPLORING AND MONETIZING THE SOCIAL NETWORK FRONTIER

A social network site is a Web-based service that lets people create a profile of themselves within that service that can be shared with others. The profile usually has biographical information, pictures, and any information the person creating it wants to share about him- or herself. There is variation from site to site in technology capabilities, but usually members can communicate with others using the site by chat, blogs, instant message, and sometimes by videoconferencing. There are social networks where the user can stay in touch with a circle of friends and make new friends. There are social networks organized around race, nationality, religious preferences, political interests, and business interests, to name a few. Hundreds of millions of people worldwide have joined one or more social networking sites. MySpace, owned by News Corp., is the largest social network with 72 million users.

In 2007, global advertising on social networking sites increased by 155% to $1.2 billion. This year, the research firm eMarketer anticipates an increase of 75%. But while a lot of money is being spent on advertising, the return on advertising so far hasn't been what was anticipated. However, Google wants to explore the revenue potential in this territory in a big way. Currently, it is trying several different approaches to reach the social networking crowd: through its own social network orkut, a deal with My Space, and the Open Social Alliance.

Google's social network site, orkut, interestingly enough, was launched in the United States with an English-only interface, but Portuguese-speaking Brazilians quickly became the dominant user group.[15]

While MySpace gets four times the traffic that Google's orkut does globally, orkut has recently surpassed MySpace traffic in China, Japan, and Latin America. In 2006 to 2007, visitors to the orkut site from China and Japan almost tripled, reaching approximately 11 million. Its Latin American traffic is double that of MySpace. Traffic sells ads for Google, although it would undoubtedly like to increase orkut's popularity in the United States and Europe, where there are richer potential shoppers to draw more advertising dollars. And while the money spent on social site networks is increasing, the ads aren't generating the sales that advertisers need to justify continuing to spend their advertising dollars on these sites indefinitely.[16]

Collaboration with the global leader MySpace is another approach Google tried. Google made a $900 advertising deal million deal with MySpace. But it hasn't been happy with the return on advertising, and it's uncertain whether it will continue with this strategy. Sergey commented in February 2008 that, "I don't think we have the killer, best way to advertise and monetize social networks yet."[17] A few months later, he told reporters that putting together the technology and the best approach to social networking advertising would take time.[18]

Like Google, other companies have been pumping money into advertising on social networks to test the waters, and not all of them are happy with the returns. Could it be that people on social networks are more interested in socializing than shopping?[19]

Another approach to capturing the attention and advertising dollars of those who use the Internet for social networking that Google and others are pursuing is increasing the opportunities of people to socialize no matter where they are on the Web. Jeff Huber, Google's senior vice president of engineering, commented that, "The web is fundamentally better when it's social; we're only just starting to see what's possible when you bring social information into different contexts on the web."[20]

In November 2007, Google announced the release of a common set of application program interfaces—or APIs—for social applications across the Web. APIs are a set of tools and protocols for building software applications. Prior to this, developers were forced to write applications using a range of different APIs so that the applications would work with particular social network sites. Now, with a common set of APIs for Web-based social applications, developers will be able to quickly develop new applications that could be used on any Web site. Programmers will be able to use the single standard to create the means for any Web site to provide the capability for users to share their interests and contacts, for example. In this fashion, the entire Web can become more social.

Developers will have a huge distribution network for the social applications they develop. Web sites adding the new social applications can attract and satisfy visitors who want to socialize with the social features on their sites. Users don't have to restrict their social interactions to social networking sites. Best of all for Google, it could help redirect social network users to the Web where Google dominates advertising, rather than having them just using the Web to primarily access their social networks.

Google created Friend Connect using the new APIs and announced a preview of how it would work on May 12, 2008. With Friend Connect, Web site owners can add a "snippet of code" to their sites and, without programming, quickly make social features available to those who visit their site. Site owners can offer their visitors the option to invite their friends to the Web site, including their friends from the social networking sites, to post messages, write reviews, and select other applications built by the OpenSocial developer community. This is another move by Google to spread the option of socializing across the entire Web.

In the press release on Friend Connect, Google summarizes its impact.

> Google Friend Connect has been developed to lower two barriers to the spread of social features across the web. First, many website owners want to add features that enable their visitors to do things with their friends, but the technology and resource hurdles have been too high. Second, people are tiring of needing to create new logins and profiles and recreate their friends lists wherever they go on the web. Google Friend Connect offers a solution to both these issues.[21]

Google is experimenting with some fascinating approaches to tapping the advertising potential of social networking. It will be interesting to see how these experiments play out in the future.

FUTURE RISKS

Most companies' annual reports to shareholders have a section on risks related to their business and industry. Many of the items listed in this section in annual reports seem somewhat boilerplate. But some of the risks discussed in Google's 2007 annual report point to some legitimate current and ongoing challenges.

The report notes that, in 2007, 48% of Google's total revenues came from international revenues. Doing business internationally is challenging for all companies because of attention that must be paid to U.S. laws and regulations as well as the laws and regulations of every country where a company is doing business. Google also notes the challenges of developing its services and products in different languages and attention to cultural differences. Add to that the higher costs of doing business internationally and the potential for political and economic instability, and Google's dependence on international sources of such a high percentage of its total revenues does seem like a genuine risk.

Google also notes in this section of the annual report the extent to which it relies on its corporate culture, which drives the innovation necessary for the company's success. Maintaining this culture as the company grows will continue to be a challenge. Recruiting the brightest and the best engineers in an industry where there is so much competition for talent will also be a challenge.

Google management acknowledges in this section of the annual report that if Google is unable "to attract and retain a substantial number of alternative device users to our web search services or if we are slow to develop products and technologies that are more compatible with non-PC communications devices, we will fail to capture a significant share of an increasingly important portion of the market for online services, which could adversely affect our business." More people are using devices such as mobile telephones, television devices, personal digital assistants to access the Internet. This means new product and technology design challenges for Google if they want to capture the market of the people accessing the Internet through non-computer devices.[22]

Finally, the risk mentioned in its annual report of losing CEO Eric Schmidt or Larry or Sergey is a serious risk. Most would not argue with the statement that they "are critical to the overall management of Google as well as the development of our technology, our culture and our strategic direction." For those of us who have followed Larry and Sergey's journey from Stanford to the present and applauded their accomplishments, we know that they are the heart and soul of Google, and the loss of either one of them would be devastating to the company and to the millions of people who rely on Google.[23]

NOTES

1. "Corporate Information: Our Philosophy," Google, http://www.google.com/corporate/tenthings.html (accessed March 23, 2008).

2. Juan Carlos Perez, "Q&A: Vint Cerf on Google's Challenges, Aspirations," *Computerworld*, November 25, 2005, http://www.computerworld.com/developmenttopics/development/story/0,10801,106535,00.html (accessed May 18, 2008).

3. "Corporate Information: Google Management," Google, http://www.google.com/corporate/execs.html#vint (accessed May 21, 2008).

4. Louise Story and Miguel Helft, "Google Buys DoubleClick for $3.1 Billion," *New York Times,* April 14, 2007, http://www.nytimes.com/2007/04/14/technology/14DoubleClick.html?ex=1334203200&en=efd4fc413df1a9aa&ei=5088 (accessed March 23, 2008).

5. Chris Taylor, "Imagining the Google Future," CNN Money.com, February 1, 2006, http://money.cnn.com/magazines/business2/business2_archive/2006/01/01/8368125/index.htm (accessed March 15, 2008).

6. YouTube's Brand Channel, http://www.youtube.com/advertise (accessed May 10, 2008).

7. "Google Announces $10 Million Android Developer Challenge," Google Press Center, November 12, 2007, http://www.google.com/intl/en/press/pressrel/20071112_android_challenge.html (accessed April 11, 2008).

8. Android Developer Challenge, http://code.google.com/android/adc.html (accessed April 11, 2008).

9. Martin H. Bosworth, "Wireless Spectrum May Hold Key to Net Neutrality," ConsumerAffairs.com, June 4, 2007, http://www.consumeraffairs.com/news04/2007/06/wireless_spectrum.html (accessed April 14, 2008).

10. Ex Parte Filing to Federal Communications Commission (FCC): Service Rules for the 690–746, 747–762, and 777–792, MHz Bands (WC Docket No. 06–150; WC Docket No. 06–129; PS, Docket No. 06–229; WT Docket No. 96–86), Electronic Filing, July 9, 2007.

11. Ibid.

12. "Google Plan Would Open TV Band for Wireless Use," *New York Times,* March 25, 2008, http://www.nytimes.com/2008/03/25/business/media/25google.html?_r=2&th&emc=th&oref=slogin&oref=slogin (accessed April 27, 2008).

13. "Google," Wikipedia, http://en.wikipedia.org/wiki/Google (accessed April 20, 2008).

14. "Yahoo! Supports OpenSocial; Yahoo!, MySpace and Google to Form Non-Profit OpenSocial Foundation," Google Press Center, March 25, 2008, http://www.google.com/intl/en/press/pressrel/20080325_opensocial.html (accessed April 29, 2008).

15. Spencer E. Ante and Catherine Holahan, "Generation MySpace Is Getting Fed Up," *BusinessWeek,* February 7, 2008, http://www.businessweek.com/magazine/content/08_07/b4071054390809.htm (accessed May 19, 2008).

16. Olga Kharif, "Google's Orkut: A World of Ambition," *BusinessWeek,* October 8, 2007, http://www.businessweek.com/technology/content/oct2007/tc2007107_530965.htm (accessed May 15, 2008).

17. Spencer E. Ante and Catherine Holahan, "Generation MySpace Is Getting Fed Up," *BusinessWeek,* February 7, 2008, http://www.businessweek.com/magazine/content/08_07/b4071054390809.htm (accessed May 19, 2008).

18. Steven Scheer and Rebecca Harrison, "Google Social Network Ad Business 'Improving': Brin," Reuters, May 15, 2008, http://www.reuters.com/article/technologyNews/idUSL1515161520080515 (accessed May 18, 2008).

19. Spencer E. Ante and Catherine Holahan, "Generation MySpace Is Getting Fed Up," *BusinessWeek,* February 7, 2008, http://www.businessweek.com/magazine/content/08_07/b4071054390809.htm (accessed May 19 2008).

20. "Google Launches OpenSocial to Spread Social Applications across the Web," Google Press Center, November 1, 2007, http://www.google.com/intl/en/press/pressrel/opensocial.html (accessed May 20, 2008).

21. "Previewing Google Friend Connect: Website Owners Can Make Any Site Social," Google Press Center, May 12, 2008, http://www.google.com/intl/en/press/annc/20080512_friend_connect.html (accessed May 20, 2008).

22. *Annual Report 2007*, Google, http://investor.google.com/documents/2007_Google_AnnualReport.html (accessed May 21, 2008).

23. Ibid.

Appendices

A: LEARNING MORE ABOUT GOOGLE

Books

Battelle, John. *The Search: How Google and Its Rivals Rewrote the Rules of Business and Transformed Our Culture* (New York: Penguin, 2005).

John Battelle is the cofounding editor of *Wired* and the founder of *The Industry Standard* and thestandard.com. *The Search* is an excellent source of background and inside stories about Google, especially in its early years. It is based on more than 350 interviews, including interviews with Larry Page, Sergey Brin, Eric Schmidt, and Google's competitors and its predecessors in the world of search.

Vise, David A., and Mark Malseed. *The Google Story: Inside the Hottest Business, Media, and Technology Success of Our Time* (New York: Random House, 2005).

David Vise is a Pulitzer Prize–winning reporter for the *Washington Post* and the author of the *New York Times* bestseller *The Bureau and the Mole* as well as other books. Mark Malseed has contributed to the *Washington Post* and the *Boston Herald*. He also provided research for Bob Woodward's recent books *Plan of Attack* and *Bush at War*. This book reads like a great story, and it is rich with research and information from interviews and access to Google folks.

Both of these books provide detailed information about Google up to 2005. A lot has happened since 2005, and the goal of the current volume is to focus on recent events that were not covered in these two books.

Online Sources

All major U.S. and worldwide newspapers as well as smaller papers cover Google. The online *New York Times* (www.nytimes.com), *Washington Post* (www.washingtonpost.com), and *San Francisco Chronicle* (www.sfgate.com) were sources I found most useful.

I found the coverage of two writers at the *New York Times* to be particularly helpful: Saul Hansell's articles in the online *New York*

Times were highly informative. He is the editor of the Bits blog and the technology coverage on nytimes.com. Miguel Helft specializes in coverage of Internet companies for the business desk of the *New York Times* from its San Francisco bureau. He earned a master's degree in computer science at Stanford; perhaps this is why he can make complex technology issues more comprehensible to the average mortal.

Online versions of *Time* magazine (www.time.com), *Forbes* (www.forbes.com), *Fortune* (www.fortune.com), and the *Wall Street Journal* (www.wsj.com) provide good coverage of Google as well, as does the CNN Web site money.cnn.com.

Google's Web Site

Google's press releases, corporate pages, and information on its products and services are almost encyclopedic resources of information (www.google.com). See Appendix B for a list of specific Google sites.

Other Online Resources

The interview with Larry and Sergey published on the Academy of Achievement Web site (www.achievement.org/autodoc/page/pag0int-1) offers some fascinating reflections on their childhoods and early aspirations.

I found it intriguing to look at online videos of Sergey and Larry to get a better sense of who they are and what they think from being able to hear their views in their own voices. This one is an inside look at Google with Larry and Sergey: www.ted.com/index.php/talks/view/id/118.

B: A SELECTED LIST OF GOOGLE WEB ADDRESSES

Blogger, http://www.blogger.com
Froogle (shopping), http://www.googleguide.com/froogle.html
Google AdWords, http://www.adwords.google.com
Google AdSense, http://www.google.com/adsense
Google Book Search, http:// books.google.com
Google Calendar, http:// www.google.com/calendar
Google Code, http://code.google.com
Google Desktop, http://desktop.google.com
Google Docs, http://www.google.com/google-d-s/tour1.html
Google Earth, http://earth.google.com
Google Groups, http://groups.google.com
Google Image Search, http://images.google.com
Google Labs, http://labs.google.com
Google Maps, http://www.maps.google.com
Google News, http://news.google.com
Google Search Appliance, www.google.com/enterprise/gsa
Google Scholar, http://scholar.google.com
Google Mobile, http://www.google.com/mobile

Google Notebook, http://www.google.com/notebook
Google Search, http://www.google.com
Google SketchUp, www.sketchup.google.com
Google Talk, http://www.google.com/talk
Google Video, http://video.google.com
Orkut (social network), http://www.orkut.com
Picasa (photo editing), http://picasa.google.com
YouTube, http://www.youtube.com

C: GOOGLE'S FINANCIAL PERFORMANCE

Table A.1
Key Financial Data for Google

	2002	2003	2004	2005	2006	2007	First Quarter 2008
Revenue	$439,508	$1,465,934	$3,189,223	$6,138,560	$10,604,917	$16,593,986	$5,186,043
Total Costs	$253,042	$1,123,470	$2,549,031	$4,121,282	$7,054,921	$11,509,586	$3,639,808
Net Profits	$186,466	$342,464	$640,142	$2,017,278	$3,549,996	$5,084,400	$1,546,235
Earnings Per Share (Basic)	$0.86	$0.77	$2.07	$5.31	$10.21	$13.53	$4.17

Source: http://investor.google.com/fin_data.html.

Figure A.1
Google Share Price, 2004 to 2007

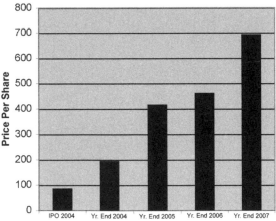

Figure A.2
Google versus S&P 500 Price Index, 2004 to 2007

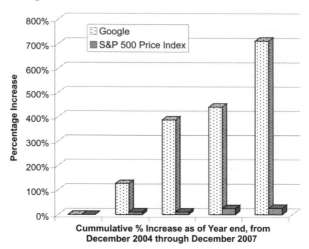

Cummulative % Increase as of Year end, from
December 2004 through December 2007

Index

About the Author

VIRGINIA SCOTT is a freelance instructional designer for colleges, universities, and private companies. Her clients have included the University of Virginia, the University of Colorado, the State of Maryland, Thomson Learning, and others. She also teaches online courses for colleges. The author of the *Agile Manager's Guide to Training for Excellence,* she holds an M.A. and M.Ed. from the University of Virginia.